MW01009286

PUBLISHER'S STATEMENT

Even before it was scheduled for publication, this book provoked enormous controversy. Some argued that it should never see the light of day.

My Return is Jack Henry Abbott's story of his involvement in the death of Richard Adan in 1981, the subsequent trial, and his intellectual, religious, and philosophical odyssey since his return to prison.

Prometheus Books agreed to publish this work primarily for its literary value, but also in order to clarify for the public record Abbott's views of the events that led to Adan's death. It is not a neutral or objective account told by an impartial bystander but the highly impassioned plea of a man involved in his own effort to exonerate himself.

In spite of its controversial nature, we consider *My Return* to be a significant book. Prometheus Books is committed to free inquiry and the airing of a wide range of views—including those with which we may differ. Though much of the public may find Jack Henry Abbott's life and his effort to clear himself in the Adan affair morally objectionable, we have given him (and Naomi Zack) the opportunity to present his version of this fascinating story. It is now up to the reader to judge the merits of the case and to weigh the moral issues involved.

Mr. Abbott will receive no remuneration for the sale of *My Return*. All royalties will become the property of the Crime Victims Compensation Board, a body charged with turning over a criminal's share in the proceeds of a publishing venture to the victims of crime.

MY RETURN

MY RETURN

JACK HENRY ABBOTT
author of In the Belly of the Beast

WITH NAOMI ZACK

PROMETHEUS BOOKS

Buffalo, New York

Photograph of the Binibon
on page 99 and the cover is
courtesy of Neal Boenzi/nyt
pictures.

Photographs on pages 96,
100, and 102 are courtesy of
Naomi Zack.

92 91 90 89 88 87   6 5 4 3 2 1

Library of Congress Cataloging-in-Publication Data

Abbott, Jack Henry, 1944-
     My return.

1. Abbott, Jack Henry, 1944-   , in fiction,
drama, poetry, etc. I. Zack, Naomi, 1945-
II. Title.
PS3551.B257M9   1987   812'.54   86-43236
ISBN 0-87975-355-2

To
Dutch Uncles

"God bless Cap'n Vere!"

CONTENTS

INTRODUCTION
by Naomi Zack

This is a book about a man who was paroled from prison to a halfway house on the Bowery in New York City. The halfway house was the Salvation Army, located across the street from the Men's Shelter for derelicts. Just before he left prison, the man wrote a book denouncing society, America, the government, the justice system, guards, and inmates, and declared himself an avowed Marxist who would welcome the violent destruction of the world as he knew it. He had obviously been in prison too long. That was not the problem, however. He had the misfortunes of being hailed a genius and of having gifts of expressing himself in language at least equal to that of writers the caliber of Albert Camus, to whom critics have compared him. That was his problem.

The prison authorities did not parole the man because they wanted to. He was paroled because his time was over and the law compelled them to parole him. His editors and literary friends were blamed for having used their influence to get him out of prison. This was not true. Norman Mailer, perhaps the most important writer in America, was singled out more prominently than anyone else as being responsible for obtaining the man's parole. The prison and parole authorities maintained a wall of silence and allowed Norman Mailer (and others) to take the "blame." This misunderstanding is addressed in the Prolegomena to the play published in this book. The man was placed in the worst halfway house in New York City. Six weeks later, an incident occurred that resulted in his being returned to prison. Thus the title of this book, *My Return*.

The incident was something ordinary, but everyone refused to understand it because everyone felt that he had refused to understand society, America, the government, the justice system, the guards, and the inmates in the book he had written in prison.

So they misunderstood the incident. Most of them *willed* the misunderstandings. What happened was simply this: The man was returning from an after-hours club with two friends who were accompanying him back to the Salvation Army; they stopped for breakfast at a small café in the Bowery neighborhood. The man had a disagreement with the night manager, and the night manager ordered him to leave and escorted him to the door. He went outside and turned back toward the door, and the night manager confronted him and ordered him not to return. He persisted in turning back toward the door, and the night manager persisted in stopping him. The night manager finally drew a knife to intimidate him, and the man stabbed the night manager one time and killed him accidentally.

That is the long and the short of it. Everyone refused to understand it. They convinced the man that he and his *prison experience* were responsible and that the night manager was not responsible.

As I have said: He *was* in prison too long. He was in prison so long that he did not understand things as profound in human affairs as how to order a meal from a French menu. He did not know the difference between a summer suit and a winter suit. It was these profound misunderstandings that helped convince his literary friends in Manhattan that nothing ordinary could happen to him. And so they speculated, and some of them *willed* not to understand what the common man in the street understood perfectly.

His misunderstandings, however, did play a role in the incident. Had he been alone he would have left the café at the first sign of trouble. Had he lived in New York City long enough he would have understood the commonness of what those outside the city think of as rude and obnoxious behavior. He would not have taken it as being especially directed toward him. Had he had more experience he would have understood that he was being ordered to leave the café. Had he had more experience he would have understood that the night manager only meant to intimidate him. This kind of misunderstanding was the kind of misunderstanding equal to not knowing he was wearing a winter suit in the summer.

He was not, however, alone in his misunderstandings. It takes two to tango, as the saying goes. The night manager had some misunderstandings also. Had he known to be more careful with strangers, he would probably not be dead today. But from his appearance, his words, his behavior, the night manager must not have realized any problem existed and that he could not handle the man in the manner he did.

The reason I draw a parallel between the inability to understand a French menu and the misunderstandings that occurred in the café is that no one admits that the night manager had a shared responsibility. Everyone now is of the opinion that the night manager had a *right* to do what he did. That is the last refuge after the facts have been ironed out. The two friends the man was with, had they been ordinary middle-class people, would have also been misunderstood. They would have suffered character assassination for having associated with him. No one mentions them, however. They would like to portray them as people with loose morals, anti-social characters, trivial thrill-seekers. It would fit the picture they have painted of the man, Jack Henry Abbott, author of *In the Belly of the Beast*. However, the friends were and are respected members of the old nobilities of France and Manila. And so they could not be used as a means of propagating the misunderstanding of the incident that night on the Bowery. Of course no one has ever suggested that it might speak well of *Jack's character* that he associated with these people. And of course I am not suggesting such a thing either, at this point in time.

I grew up in New York City and I spent most of my childhood on the Lower East Side near the Bowery. Then, as now, if you walked around on those streets unprotected at night, you could lose your life. You could get your throat cut in broad daylight if you were not careful. The danger comes from some of those who live there, and out-of-towners tend to ignore the problem until it is too late. Those from greater New York City tend to want to ignore or downplay the violence of some of these neighborhoods and to pretend that violence is exotic.

My Return comprises an appended play and writings by Jack. The appended play presents all the facts of the incident that resulted in Jack's stabbing a man one time and accidentally killing him. Because of all the prejudice that surrounds the incident, I compiled an appendix of facts to accompany the play. All of the drawings and illustrations are the work of the art department of Prometheus Books, and they are based on sketches and drawings Jack did for the play. We have related the genesis of the parts of the book in the Acknowledgments, which follows this introduction.

The purpose of the play is to exhibit on the stage the precise facts of the events inside the café and outside the café. The whole affair, from its beginning in the café to the conclusion with the night manager falling to the sidewalk, lasted only a few minutes. The attestations of the prosecutor's witnesses as to the *facts* are here recorded with minute care. The actual words that witnesses uttered are here recorded and acted out on the stage.

At Jack's trial, outside information was introduced by the prosecutor. He used information gleaned from sensationalistic magazines. He used select portions of Jack's book. He used hearsay information.

At his trial, after Jack had testified to all the facts, Jack made an effort to doubt the facts by reinterpreting them in such a way as to please all those who wanted to convince Jack that the night manager did not do what he did and that he was not even angry. That Jack should doubt himself to the point of examining his most fundamental values (and that is what actually occurred) resulted from habits of thought attributable to Socratic wisdom. It is on that point the tragedy falls into a farce, and that is why Jack titled the play *The Death of Tragedy*.

The night manager was not on trial. No outside information was introduced about him. Jack did not know him. Whether or not he knew who Jack was is still a mystery. It was known in the neighborhood that Jack was a celebrity staying at the Salvation Army, however.

All that is relevant are the facts of what took place at the café that night. And that is all we have reduced to dramatic form. Therefore, since the play neglects the irrelevant parts of the trial, it is not an accurate portrayal of the trial. But it is an accurate portrayal of all the evidence of what took place at the café that night. Fate is stronger than the machinations of mortals.

Jack has written open letters to a few writers, whom (with the exception of William Styron) he has corresponded with privately in the past. These are published in the Men of Letters chapter. They appear here for the first time and were never sent to the correspondents. The letters speak for themselves. The letters are not about prison this time. There are nine letters, including an "epistle." The epistle is distinguished because it contains autobiographical material and because it is the longest letter in the book. It is also the last letter. Jack wrote it as a memoir in March of 1986, and he has chosen to publish it here in this form. The views and theories he expresses in the Men of Letters section are not my views because I do not fully understand them. But I do know he has taken a view of the world from a position no one else has ever attained in literature. His thoughts are the more astounding because, except for the epistle, they were all dictated to me in the visiting room in prison over a period of ten days. The letters, including the epistle, have not been edited by anyone.

I came into this in the early part of 1983. I had just completed producing a video documentary and I was thinking about starting a new project. I had several ideas, and a colleague of mine suggested doing the "Jack Henry Abbott Story" from the perspective of those who are the victims both of crime and the justice system. I began contacting people and gathering data and outside facts. I had heard all the rumors that were abroad in what people were saying. I am a trained philosopher, and I had read Jack's book *In the Belly of the Beast*. It was clear to me that Dante's doctrine that no one could ever survive to describe the *Inferno* was refuted by Jack's book. It was not what he wrote but what he brought to the writing of it. The *pathos* of a poet makes particularities irrelevant because it transcends mundane facts with universal truths. I am not knowledgeable about prison conditions. It was his mind, his striving to be a scholar, that gripped me.

In my investigation, I began to sense a total disregard for the truth, because what was being said about the facts had nothing to do with representing the truth at all: The facts tapered into a sublated cesspool of disharmonic slander and character defamation, a total will to chaos and misunderstanding.

I began to abandon the project because it was too murky. Then I decided to review the trial records and to let that be the decisive factor of whether or not I would continue. I contacted a lawyer who had known Jack personally for more than ten years. His name was given to me by a hostile interested party. I had several discussions with the lawyer, and he sent me a copy of the trial transcript.

The lawyer finally put me into direct contact with Jack. Obviously, this book has been the result. All the rest of it—the details of our joint investigation, the expenditures in time and money, the frustrations—all of this is not important anymore. The bottom line is that any lawyer who diligently attempts to obtain a new trial for Jack, or helps him in any way, will risk his entire practice in the justice system and will earn himself the enmity of other lawyers. Jack had the temerity, in a remark or two in his first book, to appear ungrateful to lawyers in general.

Jack was acquitted of murder and found guilty of manslaughter, which carries a sentence of two to six years imprisonment. But he was sentenced to life imprisonment. The parole board will never let him out of prison because of *In the Belly of the Beast*. At this writing, he is scheduled for his first hearing before the parole board in the year 2001.

Mailer once wrote that he loves Jack for surviving and for learning to use words as well as he does. He also wrote that Jack had torn the bones of culture with his teeth but had not tasted the soup. Jack has had a hard time of it; but, over the years, he has finally tasted the soup. I care for Jack's freedom because I believe he is one of the most promising young philosophers so far to appear in my generation. But he has paid—more than any man today who has been convicted of manslaughter—for the events of that fateful night (over five years ago) both in the time he has so far served and in his dangerous circumstances in prison. No one serves fifteen years to life imprisonment for manslaughter.

May 1987

ACKNOWLEDGMENTS

Practically all of the dialogue in *The Death of Tragedy* was gleaned from court records, formal statements in the presence of lawyers, and public sources in the publishing media. The bare dialogue was originally extracted from these sources and sequentially arranged by Dr. Naomi Zack. In the final draft, I created the play around the dialogue. It is a product of our joint collaboration. All the letters in the *Men of Letters* section are letters I wrote especially for this book.

J. A.

The original diagrams and sketches in the Appendix were the work of Jack Abbott. The photographs were selected from a series taken in several excursions into the neighborhood of the Bowery, where the Salvation Army halfway house and the restaurant were located. The information contained in the Appendix was gleaned from a number of sources, including interviews over the past several years. I compiled and wrote the original material in the Appendix and we placed it in its present form to offer background information and other supporting materials for the play.

N. Z.

We wish to express our heart-felt thanks to all those whose warm cooperation and encouragement made this work possible.

Among them, Larry Frost and Al Maxwell, private investigators in Manhattan who (working independently) provided a fruitful source of information. Peter Manso has offered a wealth of information concerning police conduct and other matters; Seymour Morganstern, who with his attorney conducted the formal transcribed interviews of trial jurors and inspired Dr. Zack to arrange the first draft of the dialogue in the play; James Long, the attorney in Albany, whose advice and encouragement was always welcomed, made a thorough appraisal of the trial records.

We wish to thank George Griffin and Ruby Katsouli for their openness in discussing their experiences in this matter; William Blunt and Michael Lucas, trial jurors, for their courage in coming forward—and many others too numerous to name.

Jack H. Abbott
Naomi Zack

PART ONE

The Death of Tragedy

Just as Greek sailors in the reign of Tiberius once heard on a lonesome island the soul-shaking cry, Great Pan is Dead! so the Hellenic world was now pierced by the grievous lament: Tragedy is dead! Poetry has perished with her! Away with you, pale meager epigones! Away to Hell that you may for once eat your fill of the crumbs of our former masters!

—Nietzsche

PROLEGOMENA TO ANY FUTURE METATHEATRE*
My Parole from Prison to New York

How I received my parole

In October 1978 the U.S. Parole Commission granted me a parole. I was at that time a prisoner at Lompoc Federal Prison in California.

No one knew I was corresponding with Norman Mailer.

My parole was set for June 1980.

In July 1979, I was given a disciplinary report for alleged involvement in an inmate work strike, and I was transferred to Marion Federal Prison in Illinois.

I was locked in a cell in punitive segregation. I was never taken out of segregation. The segregation units were on one hunger strike after another, and individuals were destroying their individual isolation cells. I was never in the regular inmate population. I was always locked in an individual cell. It was the prison "hole."

In Marion Federal Prison I accumulated six more disciplinary reports for allegedly inciting "inmate demonstrations" and for alleged individual assaults on gangs of armed prison guards.

In May 1980 I submitted the completed manuscript of my book *In the Belly of the Beast* to an editor.

A parole recision hearing was held in August 1980, and the U.S. Parole Commission inflicted the maximum penalty on me by extending my parole date fourteen months (from June 1980 to August 1981). I was given a sixty-day sanction on each of the seven disciplinary reports. It was the absolute maximum.

The U.S. Parole Commission acts under guidelines set by the U.S. Congress. Under the guidelines the U.S. Parole Commission was not

---

* metatheatre (met'·a·the'·a·tre: *meta* = after, beyond; *theatre* from Gr. *theatron,* akin to *theasthia, thea, thauma, theoros, theo: theatron* = an edifice for performances, etc.) Def.: 1. The world conceived of as a stage. 2. Suffering conceived metaphysically, as imparting divine attributes (Nietzsche, *Beyond Good and Evil,* aphorism 229). 3. Confer with the critical essay by Lionel Abel, *Metatheatre* (New York: Hill and Wang, 1963) for related discussion.

empowered to do more than extend my parole date a maximum of sixty days for each disciplinary report. This is because none of the accusations against me could result in further violation of federal law or further prosecution.

In February 1981, I was removed from Marion Federal Prison and returned to the Utah State Prison and held there in Maximum Security (as a *federal prisoner*) because it was determined my life was in danger at Marion Federal Prison.

How my Utah sentence was terminated

In March 1971 (ten years previously) I had escaped from Maximum Security at the Utah State Prison. Maximum Security is a separate prison facility outside the regular prison perimeter.

A few days after I was returned to Utah State Prison, I was taken out of the prison and placed in the county jail to face a charge of prison escape, which carried a penalty of ten years' imprisonment. The prison authorities pressed charges to have me put on trial for escape. The court ruled that the prison authorities had denied me a fair trial, a right guaranteed under the federal "Fair and Speedy Trial Act" of the U.S. Congress, by waiting ten years to begin proceedings against me. The State of Utah and the prison authorities did not want to release me.

In 1973, while I was in Leavenworth Federal Prison in Kansas, the Utah State Legislature repealed the special convict laws under which I had been sentenced to three-to-twenty years for violation of a law entitled *Assault By Convict Without Malice Aforethought* (Utah Code Annotated, 1956).

I was not notified of this legislative action, however. A new sentencing structure was introduced, modifying my sentence of three-to-twenty years to somewhere in the range of three years *minimum* to ten years *maximum*. Indeterminate sentencing was abolished. I had served more than eight years before I escaped. The director of the Utah Board of Corrections, Mr. Weber, informed me that the modification in my case could not exceed the more than eight years I had already served. He informed me that the Board of Corrections was to hold a hearing and formally terminate my sentence to coincide with my federal parole date. My time was served.

In April 1981 this was done. It was decided that Utah had no further claim on me. Federal law required that all prisoners to be released on parole were to be kept in a halfway house at least ninety days prior to the inmate's parole. It was arranged that I be placed in the Salvation Army on the Bowery in Manhattan on June 5, 1981, to await my August 27, 1981, parole release date.

On that day, I walked out of prison from punitive isolation in Maximum Security.

How I went to New York

At the formal hearing to terminate my sentence, one of the four members of the Board of Corrections raised a concern that I might seek vengeance if I were to reside in Utah. He was the youngest man on the Board. He neither knew me nor had access to my prison record of ten years earlier, since it had been destroyed. Another member of the Board was curious about the financial terms of my publishing contract. That was the extent of the hearing.

In 1962, while I was at the Davis County Jail, the county sheriff (a forty-year-old rancher) told my judge I had threatened him and his deputies. That was done in the wake of my arm being broken. In my prison commitment papers there was a notice to the Board of Corrections to the effect that if a parole hearing was held before five years (the expiration of my sentence) the Sheriff's Department of Davis County was to be notified in advance in order to appear and contest the idea of ever paroling me. That notice was still in the records, and Utah's intention was to be sure I was not given a federal parole to Utah.

I assured the Board of Corrections that I did not plan to live in Utah and that I would never return to the state under any circumstances.

The Board formally terminated my sentence to coincide with my federal parole from a halfway house in New York.

The only question to be determined before I appeared before the Board of Corrections was where I was to take up residency. My federal conviction was in Denver, Colorado, and the federal court there had jurisdiction over my parole.

I was opposed to staying in Denver, and referred to my letters of recommendation. A letter from Norman Mailer, and letters from two prominent editors, had assured the Board of my possibilities of earning a living as a writer in New York. It was on the basis of this that I was placed in a New York City halfway house instead of a halfway house in Denver.

None of the authorities involved in this matter communicated with Norman Mailer or anyone other than my relatives. They merely accepted the letters at face value and consulted me and my relatives. Mailer's name was never mentioned nor was anyone's name who had written to the Board. Besides my literary "sponsors" six ordinary people also wrote letters.

The federal parole officer, a middle-aged man who had been in this profession most of his life, predicted there would be trouble when he learned which halfway house I was to be placed in.

The concern was always only whether I could support myself as a writer and whether I would be among friends and not be isolated in New York.

There was no question as to whether or not I would be paroled. Not to have paroled me would have violated the law.

Had my friends not written to the Board, I would have been placed in a halfway house in Denver and not in Manhattan.

But I would certainly have been paroled in any case.

Norman Mailer's letter did not result in my parole.

The Death of Tragedy*
[A Play in Three Acts]

* * *

The protagonist must defend his actions with arguments and counter-arguments and in the process risks the loss of our tragic pity. Philosophic thought overgrows art and compels it to cling close to the trunk of dialectic—for our protagonist must be a dialectician now; now there must be a necessary, visible connection between virtue and knowledge, faith and morality; now justice is degraded to the superficial and insolent principle of "poetic justice."

Virtue is knowledge; man sins only from ignorance; he who is virtuous is happy. In these basic forms of optimism lies the death of tragedy.

—Nietzsche

by
Jack Henry Abbott and Naomi Zack, Ph.D.

Dedication

This play is dedicated to enlightenment and free spirits everywhere.

---

* Tragedy derives from the Greek *tragoidia,* combining the roots *tragos* + *oide* (*tragos* = he-goat; *oide* = song). In his great essay, *The Birth of Tragedy,* Nietzsche associated the death of tragedy with the rise of Socratic wisdom and the abandonment of *tragic wisdom.* Confer with the critical essay by George Steiner, *The Death of Tragedy* (New York: Knopf, 1961), for contrary discussion.

Characters

JACK H. ABBOTT, *the defendant*	FOHSTA, *witness*
VERONIQUE DE ST. ANDRÉ, *his*	DEFENSE LAWYER
friend; witness	PROSECUTOR
SUSAN ROXAS, *his friend; witness*	LT. MAJESKY, *detective*
RICHARD ADAN, *night manager*	BLUNT, *juror*
of café	LUCAS, *juror*
WAITER, *witness*	LEADER *and* CHORUS
LARSEN, *witness*	ABBOTT CHARACTER
KATHY, *witness*	*Café customers and pedestrians*

Preface

The closing address of the Prosecutor at the actual trial has been dramatically reduced. Neither the Prosecutor's speeches nor the Judge's statements at sentencing have lost their meaning. Most of the lines are direct quotations.

The closing address in the play was not the closing address of the actual trial lawyer but my own defense. The dialogue of the Defense Lawyer in the play is accurate and taken from the trial transcript.

Lt. Majesky's statements were not delivered at the trial but in recorded interviews following the trial. His statements were worked into the play to further dramatize facts obscured by the publicity that surrounded the case.

Other than these exceptions, all of the words of the characters who speak here are exact quotations from the trial testimony and appear in accurate order of the unfolding of the trial.

The statements of Mr. Lucas and Mr. Blunt (the Jurors) were given under formal conditions after the trial. Mr. Lucas' regrets were expressed, in fact, hours after delivering a verdict that clearly went against his conscience. The Defense Lawyer was fired immediately following my sentencing, having been notified in advance (after the verdict).

All the dialogue (except my testimony) is the testimony of witnesses for the Prosecution. This includes the testimony of Susan Roxas. Her testimony, as with the testimony of the rest of the witnesses, was not injurious. She is still a friend. Susan and Veronique were both twenty-four years of age at the time.

All the witnesses appearing in this play appeared as government witnesses for the Prosecutor. None of them contradicted the account given in this play except for certain uncorroborated emotional "inferences" made by one hostile witness. (The rest of his testimony is presented in the play.)

Therefore, Act Two is not as it appears: it is *not* the actual Defense Lawyer's defense. It was necessary to employ the portions from my trial lawyer's questioning of me for the simple reason that the Prosecutor never questioned me about the crime I was on trial for. Had the Prosecutor questioned me about the crime I was on trial for, we would have used my responses to his questions for the play and entirely disregarded the trial lawyer's questioning. The most fruitful responses came from the witnesses' responses to questions directed by the Prosecutor.

Veronique, a French citizen, returned to Paris and refused to appear, stating that "Jack is my friend." French procedure in criminal prosecutions is radically different from that in America. Veronique thought she would not be allowed to speak to me or my lawyer and would be tricked into harming me. This is why she refused to return to America. The dialogue attributed to Veronique was taken from Susan's testimony, where she quoted Veronique.

*   *   *

In the style of the Alexandrian, we have included information and briefs in the Appendix, along with drawings, which we include for two classes of reader: those who cannot read and those who cannot act.

The play is footnoted.

The CHORUS resurrects, in an appropriate manner, the Furies.

ACT I
Prologue

The Binibon café, on the corner of Second Avenue and Fifth Street, at about five o'clock in the morning in July 1981.

A wide sidewalk and Second Avenue to its left run from front to rear at the left of the stage. A lamppost with signs rises from the corner of the sidewalk. This part of the stage is brightly lit. At the far left a middle-aged newspaper lady, KATHY, *sits on a stoop below an arched doorway. Across the front of the stage, in shadow, is a narrow sidewalk parallel with Fifth Street. A pile of garbage bags and boxes lies to the right, while toward the corner with Second Avenue are a tree, a fire hydrant, and a small low dumpster.*

Behind a mere suggestion of walls (facing Fifth Street) and bay windows (facing Second Avenue), the Binibon café takes up most of the stage, from far right to left of center. In the front center of the café is a long bench, followed by two straggling rows of small square tables and scattered chairs, five tables to each row. The two tables to the far right are somewhat distanced from the others, and busy cleaning one of them is a WAITER, *wearing a white t-shirt. A passageway behind the tables leads to the door, which opens outward onto Second Avenue. In the rear right corner of the café is the square kitchen, hidden from view. A door in the kitchen's far left wall leads to the rear of the café.*

A service counter, with four stools, and shelving on the wall behind it fill up the rest of the back of the café. * *Standing behind the counter is the café's night manager,* ADAN, *wearing a black t-shirt. He is five feet, nine inches tall and weighs one-hundred-and-seventy pounds.*

The CHORUS LEADER *enters from the left and speaks in modulated tones. She is dressed in a black robe with a cowl concealing her face.*

LEADER
The café before you is located on the Bowery, on the Lower East Side of

---

*Cf. Appendix I, Section 1, A, B, C.

Manhattan. It is July 1981—the hottest day in twenty years in New York. Men sleep, beg, and live on the sidewalks in this neighborhood. Many of them are heroin addicts, thieves, winos. Most are derelicts of all descriptions. It is a poor, predominantly black and Puerto Rican neighborhood. In Manhattan, seventeen people are being killed in acts of violence, and most of them die here, on the Bowery. More crimes of violence are being committed on the Lower East Side of Manhattan than in any other place in America. The three people who are about to appear are coming from an all-night outing at a nightclub in the SoHo district of Manhattan. They are stopping for breakfast before going home. They have walked quite a distance. Watch carefully. Watch what happens. Watch the hands move on the clock of existence.

JACK H. ABBOTT, VERONIQUE DE ST. ANDRÉ, and SUSAN ROXAS enter from the rear and walk down the sidewalk of Second Avenue. ABBOTT is wearing blue jeans, tan suede walking shoes, and a long-sleeved pullover shirt with horizontal stripes of white and beige. VERONIQUE is wearing jeans, sandals, and a white blouse. SUSAN is wearing dark slacks, sandals, and a white blouse. They are in a festive mood, talking inaudibly but in an animated way. SUSAN and VERONIQUE seem oblivious to the surroundings. The group occasionally pauses, self-absorbed, and then continues. They laugh. Once or twice ABBOTT looks cautiously around him. The group approaches the café door.

LEADER
The cowl falls, revealing her head before she speaks.
Let me introduce them. Neither of the young women is an American citizen. One of them is from Paris, France. She is the daughter of a French count. Her family is famous in France. The other young woman is in her last year at Barnard College for women. She belongs to one of the oldest families in the Philippines. She is from Manila. Her grandfather was once the president of her country. The man they are with is an American, raised in the West. In Utah. He is thirty-seven years old but looks younger than his years. He is recovering from a long hunger strike. He weighs one-hundred-and-twenty-two pounds. He has been out of prison exactly six weeks. He's been placed in a halfway house less than two blocks away, at the Salvation Army, on the Bowery.

ABBOTT and VERONIQUE freeze in position while SUSAN speaks.

SUSAN
With a marked foreign accent.
Veronique and I were sort of tipsy. We laughed and were singing in the streets sometimes. We were walking Jack home. Veronique said, "Let's get a bite to eat." So we decided to have something to eat in the café. So we went in.

ABBOTT opens the café door, and the women enter. He follows. The threesome sit at the second table to the right in the front row. VERONIQUE sits on the bench, with her back to the audience. SUSAN sits on a chair on the right, ABBOTT on the left. While they act out the ritual of seating themselves, the LEADER continues.

LEADER
It is about five o'clock in the morning. There are ten to fifteen people in the café, sitting at tables singly or in pairs, and on the stools at the counter. Only three people are working in the café. One of them is the cook in the kitchen, out of sight. One of them, the one wearing the white t-shirt, is the only waiter. The other one, the one wearing the black t-shirt, is the night manager.

ADAN comes from around the counter with three menus and drops them in a stack on the table where ABBOTT and the women have sat down. As soon as the menus smack the table, the LEADER, startled, reacts.

LEADER
Changes tone. She draws herself up and speaks in sharp, angry, stentorian tones.
I am the Judge! The State of New York versus Jack Henry Abbott!
She makes a flourish, offering the stage to the audience, and then exits stiffly.

ADAN puts his hands on his hips. SUSAN and VERONIQUE each pick up a menu; then ABBOTT looks up at ADAN and speaks to him. ABBOTT does not pick up a menu. ADAN places his left hand on ABBOTT's right shoulder, interrupting ABBOTT, and speaks directly to ABBOTT's upturned face. ADAN looks annoyed. AB-BOTT shrugs his right shoulder and tries to pull it away from

ADAN'S hand, but ADAN firmly refuses to remove his hand. Ig-noring ABBOTT, ADAN looks at SUSAN and speaks, but she does not notice. She is looking at her menu and speaking to VERONI-QUE. As ABBOTT makes another effort to move away from ADAN's hand, SUSAN's and VERONIQUE's attention shifts to ADAN. They look curiously at ADAN while ABBOTT squirms. ADAN, when ABBOTT tries for the last time (unsuccessfully) to pull away, points (and speaks) with his right arm extended at the WAITER, who is busy wiping off the table to the right. Then he places his right hand on his hip and looks at SUSAN and VERONI-QUE, amused, as the two women crane to look over at the WAITER and signal to him. The WAITER looks up, leaves his spot, and walks over to the table. ABBOTT is looking from ADAN to the WAITER, from SUSAN to VERONIQUE—bewildered. As the WAITER arrives, ADAN removes his hand from ABBOTT's shoulder and steps backward two steps, as if he is letting ABBOTT go. Then ADAN turns and walks over to the end of the counter. He stands there with his elbow resting on the counter and surveys the customers in the café in the way of proprietors. When he walks away, SUSAN, VERONIQUE, and ABBOTT shrug. SUSAN turns to address the audience, while the others freeze.

SUSAN
And Jack ordered some eggs. And Veronique and I were talking a long time over what we wanted to eat, discussing it.

While SUSAN and VERONIQUE begin talking to each other, ABBOTT speaks to the WAITER, who stands and writes on a pad of paper. ABBOTT never touches his menu. The WAITER stands behind SUSAN in the manner of a correct waiter, waiting quietly for the women to speak to him. He is watching and listening to them. ABBOTT glances at SUSAN and VERONIQUE and then, resting his hands on the table top, sits back in his chair, waiting. After surveying the customers, ADAN shifts his attention back to their table. Then he moves around loitering. ABBOTT's attention wanders, and he glances over at ADAN. And ADAN, as soon as ABBOTT's face turns in his direction, stops and speaks across the distance. And as he speaks, he folds his arms across his chest and shifts his feet so that he stands facing ABBOTT squarely. Ignoring him, ABBOTT turns his head quickly to the women and sits up in his chair. SUSAN and VERONIQUE are absorbed in discussing the menu, pointing at items and debating. ABBOTT relaxes again and sits back in his chair. ADAN does not move a muscle. He speaks again, but ABBOTT does not turn. ADAN waits, staring, without moving or changing his posture. VERONIQUE begins speaking to the WAITER, who begins writing on his pad. ABBOTT is totally relaxed, and when SUSAN speaks to the WAITER, ABBOTT's attention moves back in the direction where ADAN is standing. As ABBOTT's head turns and focuses on ADAN, he tenses involuntarily, as if doing a double take. Seeing this, ADAN makes the same remark. This time ABBOTT speaks back to him. ADAN repeats what he said. ADAN unfolds his arms. ABBOTT rises. ADAN begins to walk toward him. Seeing ABBOTT move from the table and approach him, he stops and waits with his hands on his hips. The women pay no attention to this. ADAN steps back and resumes a position at the end of the counter, with his arms folded and his feet standing squarely. He watches ABBOTT's face. He frowns—impatient. He is not smiling, nor does he have a quizzical look on his face. He is staring. ABBOTT stops before him and makes a remark. They freeze.

SUSAN
Turning to the audience.
And I noticed Jack talking to the manager. I noticed they looked as though they were arguing. I remember wondering why Jack looked so angry.

LEADER
From off-stage, shouting loudly.
Abbott's lawyer objects to what the witness was wondering! Abbott's lawyer objects!

SUSAN
Continuing, cautiously.
And so I turned my head. I paid it no mind. I turned to Veronique, and we started talking.*

---

*In her testimony Susan insisted that Abbott was sober all evening and was not intoxicated in the café. She also insisted that Abbott did not excuse himself from the table to use the restroom but to speak to Adan. Susan was never in com-

*As the women talk, ADAN, staring at ABBOTT, makes a sharp
reply, not moving a muscle. ABBOTT shrugs and turns away, and
as he takes a step back toward his table, ADAN (still staring, not
moving a muscle) makes another remark. ABBOTT stops in mid-
stride and turns toward him quickly. ADAN stiffens, unfolds his
arms, and puts his hands on his hips, again making several sharp
remarks. He has an annoyed, defiant look on his face. The actors
freeze while the WAITER turns to face the audience.*

WAITER
I was going back and forth serving them. And I noticed that he had gotten
up and he was talking to the night manager. The night manager was in
front of him, sort of blocking him. They were very close together and they
were both talking in rough, hard tones. I don't know what was said, but I
heard him say to the night manager: "Don't tell me what to do."

*The WAITER turns and goes upstage toward ABBOTT's left.
ABBOTT glances at him and stops him with an outstretched arm.
The WAITER stops, distracted, and ABBOTT speaks as he watches
ADAN. ADAN turns abruptly and steps behind the counter.
ABBOTT and the WAITER watch him, while ABBOTT continues
to speak to the WAITER. ADAN has his back to them and is doing
something on a shelf against the wall. He turns. The WAITER
shrugs his shoulders, steps backward, and turns to face the audience.
The others freeze.*

WAITER
Both of them had very serious faces on. Neither of them were smiling.
Both of them were serious. Abbott said, "You don't have to push me." It
was a common thing for the night manager to tell a customer to leave if it
appears he is making trouble.*

*The WAITER walks to the far right table. ADAN, with his right
hand in his pocket, walks up to ABBOTT and hits ABBOTT's chest
with his own, deliberately. ADAN speaks rapidly, and his left hand
points at the door of the café. ABBOTT steps back when ADAN*

---

munication with Abbott or anyone who knew Abbott (or any representative of
Abbott). She was a state witness.
*Cf. Appendix II, Section 4.

bumps him and then looks over at the WAITER, who looks away. Deliberately ignoring all of this, the WAITER walks meekly and quickly away, toward the kitchen. SUSAN keeps glancing over at ABBOTT's back and at ADAN. ADAN walks to the door, and ABBOTT follows closely. SUSAN sees this and looks at VERONI-QUE curiously. They then ignore it and continue to talk. The other actors freeze as the WAITER speaks.

WAITER
Abbott said, "Alright, we'll go outside." They walked outside, the two of them. It was the first time I recall him going outside like that. I had only been working there one month. I did not know him personally.

ADAN opens the door, and ABBOTT walks outside onto the side-walk. ADAN is holding the door open with his left hand, so that he is standing just outside the café. His right hand is still in his pocket. ABBOTT stops and turns toward ADAN. ADAN pantomimes ushering in a customer, who passes between him and ABBOTT. From now until the end of the scene, their actions, as well as those of the other actors, continue through the following dialogue, keeping pace with the witnesses' descriptions.

KATHY
Rousing herself to speak.
I was sitting on the stoop across the street from the café. I saw the manager come out first. Then I seen Jack come out. Then I seen a tall blond guy; he was like in the doorway. After they came out of the café, they went around the corner.

ADAN speaks and shoos ABBOTT on with his left hand. He releases the door, steps toward ABBOTT. ABBOTT turns and walks several steps away from ADAN. He then stops and turns to speak to ADAN. Again, ADAN speaks, walks toward ABBOTT, shoos him with his left hand. ABBOTT turns and walks to the corner of the block. ADAN, now standing where ABBOTT just stood, repeats the same behavior: he speaks, walks toward ABBOTT, shoos him on with his left hand.

The WAITER comes to the café window by the door, watching.

From the orchestra, LARSEN approaches the stage in line with the sidewalk on Second Avenue. He is about thirty-five years old, emotional. As he walks toward ADAN, he speaks in excited tones.

LARSEN

I was across the street, walking up toward Fifth Street. I suddenly became aware—I think because of the animated movement of the two figures rounding the corner across the street from me. I was still about twenty-five feet from the curb. About one-hundred feet from them. I noticed on the part of the one who got stabbed there was some sort of gesturing going on to the front of his body. No, no dramatic movements, but some kind of gesturing.

ABBOTT turns the corner and walks right, stops (startled) between the tree and the hydrant and turns to face ADAN.* ADAN is standing on the corner that ABBOTT just left. ABBOTT does not move. He shouts. ADAN shoos him away with his left hand. ABBOTT withdraws a knife from under his belt. He holds it with his right hand in full view. He shouts again at ADAN. He takes one hesitant step forward. ADAN, taking his right hand out of his pocket, rushes at ABBOTT. ABBOTT crouches low, steps forward, and blocks ADAN'S upraised arm with his left. At the same time, ABBOTT swings his knife and comes into an upright position. He stabs ADAN in the chest. ADAN stops instantly, still upright.

LARSEN

Excitedly.

At a certain point very early on in terms of my watching this, the one who was stabbed went into reverse, so to speak. I'd say at the time they were only two or three paces off Second Avenue, on Fifth Street. He started walking backwards, not turning around, not pausing, not stopping.

ABBOTT pulls back the knife buried in ADAN. He backs up, shouting at ADAN. ADAN brings both hands to his chest and steps backwards. ABBOTT lowers his knife and walks toward ADAN. ADAN'S head is erect; his back is stiffly erect. It is as if he were marching erect and backwards. ABBOTT follows beside him, gazing at him, surprised.†

---

*Cf. Appendix I, Section 2, C.   †Cf. Appendix I, Section 2, B.

LARSEN
More excitedly as he comes closer to the corner.
He walked backwards several paces, at which point the other man from some—Well, I had basically been watching the one walking backwards. So I'm not sure whether in the interim the other man had not moved from where I had seen him stop. My attention became riveted on him because his arm swung out and I saw what looked like a knife.

At the corner, ABBOTT shifts the knife to his left hand and reaches with his right to stop ADAN from walking onto Second Avenue. ADAN backs away. ABBOTT steps back and tries to conceal his presence by pressing stiffly against the wall of the café. But it is pointless.

LARSEN
Passing between ABBOTT and ADAN and staring at ABBOTT.
He rebounded or recoiled, pulled back to somewhere close and got himself into a solid stance and, with his hands in front of him, taunted the wounded man in a very loud voice.*

While LARSEN passes him, ABBOTT puts the knife back in his waistband and shouts and gestures for others to stop ADAN. ADAN continues walking backwards toward the traffic on Second Avenue. ABBOTT cautiously moves out, dazed, onto Second Avenue.

KATHY
They came back and the night manager was holding his chest. Someone screamed. I don't know who.

ADAN, three feet from the curb on Second Avenue, turns on his heel, making a ninety-degree turn exactly as a soldier turns and, still upright with both hands on his chest, marches backwards past the café, close to the curb. As he turns and marches upstage, ABBOTT follows him, stunned.

WAITER
I was looking out the bay window. I watched him coming by from the corner and fall to the sidewalk.

---

*Cf., Appendix II, Section 2.

ADAN passes FOHSTA, who is walking down the sidewalk in the opposite direction.

FOHSTA
I was walking downtown, by the café. He was coming toward me, backing up like he had gotten punched, holding his chest. Someone screamed. I heard one scream.

ADAN falls face-down on the sidewalk, three feet from the curb. His feet point upstage, his head downstage. LARSEN glances toward the body; FOHSTA stops. ABBOTT walks over and stares at the body as it lies on the sidewalk. From the rear upstage, the CHORUS—four actresses in black robes—approach and crowd around the body, behaving like shocked pedestrians.

FOHSTA
He fell. He was backing right past me.

LARSEN
Excitedly.
I don't know how many steps he took before he collapsed to the pavement. Abbott walked up and looked at him as he laid on the sidewalk. Abbott's hands were empty. Then he backed away.

ABBOTT backs away a few feet from the body, turns, and walks quickly to the café door. He opens it. SUSAN and VERONIQUE look up at him.* He signals them to come. They rise and walk to the corner. ABBOTT speaks to them.

FOHSTA
He was with two ladies, and he said to me: "Don't fuck with me." They was moving away.

ABBOTT and the two women turn right at the corner and stop.

SUSAN
We said, "Run." And he started to run and then he made a motion, like throwing something down. And then he ran.

---

*Susan and Veronique were still waiting for the food they ordered to be served to them.

ABBOTT turns from the women and begins to run to the right. He pauses, pulls out the knife, throws it to the sidewalk, and exits running. At the same time, the other actors freeze, except the CHORUS, which as a group moves downstage.

CHORUS
Chanting.
Run! Run! Run!

Daylight floods the scene—glaring—and then dims into blackness.*

---

*Cf., Appendix I, Section 2, A, for a complete description of the movements inside and outside the café.

ACT II
The Trial

Throughout this act ABBOTT sits on a stool in the center. Scenes occur to the right and the left of the stage around him. He is basically on a witness stand, which begins as a forum. The stage around him is as dark as possible. Use appropriate lighting to illuminate him without lighting the whole stage. A spotlight itself is not appropriate—the lighting angles can shift, even from the foot of the stage. Also the tints of light. Color speaks.

As each scene is over, it falls into darkness and the props are removed and props for the new scene are put into place.

In these scenes ABBOTT CHARACTER appears as ABBOTT narrates. ABBOTT CHARACTER has dialogue as well, synchronized with ABBOTT's narrative.

There are basically four scenes, one leading into the other. The act opens with ABBOTT being assailed by the CHORUS, for the first scene. This scene closes when the LEADER drives away the CHORUS, and the right side of the stage is lighted up to reveal in obscurity a desk and the faceless DEFENSE LAWYER, who asks questions that ABBOTT responds to. SUSAN and VERONIQUE enter (in this scene), standing appearances on the left side of stage, until the act progresses to scene three, the scene at the table cued when ABBOTT says, "We took a table by the wall. . . ." At this point, the left side of the stage lights up brightly to reveal a small square table, with three actors seated at it: VERONIQUE, SUSAN, and the ABBOTT CHARACTER. This scene includes the actor playing ADAN and the actor playing the WAITER. ABBOTT'S narration is in response to questions and is actual dialogue taken from the trial transcripts. All dialogue comes verbatim from the trial transcript.

When this scene by the table is over (props are removed in the darkness), focus shifts to ABBOTT and the DEFENSE LAWYER, for the closing scene.

ABBOTT continues the dialogue with the DEFENSE LAW-YER. When ABBOTT says, "Did I do something wrong?" light on the left side of the stage goes on again, revealing the ABBOTT

CHARACTER and ADAN confronting each other. The WAITER plays a role here as well. ABBOTT narrates. The scene continues until the end of ABBOTT's testimony.

The act finishes with the light going out on this (last) scene and with the rest of the figures in the act appearing and disappearing stage-left.

Scene 1

On center stage, ABBOTT sits on a stool under a glaring light. Behind him in the shadows and partially surrounding him is the CHORUS, all in black, with the CHORUS LEADER in the center. In her hand the LEADER holds a copy of In the Belly of the Beast. *The CHORUS here behaves as accusers, pointing at, ridiculing AB-BOTT. Primitive percussion instruments accompany the CHORUS.*

Opening Chorus

LEADER
Did you write this book? Did you write *In the Belly of the Beast*? Did you sing this goat-song you call a book?

CHORUS 1
New York *SoHo News.*

CHORUS 2
Jack Abbott has denounced his country! He is a traitor!

CHORUS 3
Los Angeles Times.

CHORUS 4
Jack Abbott is a dirty Communist!

CHORUS 2
Traitor!

CHORUS 1 *and* CHORUS 2
Traitor! Traitor!

CHORUS 3 *and* CHORUS 4
Anti-Christ! Anti-Christ!

CHORUS 1
He has laid his cards on the table!

CHORUS 3
Anyone who tries to help him will be dragged to hell with him!

LEADER
When we get done with you, Jack Abbott, you won't have enough brains
left to count your toes.

ABBOTT
Distraught.
Who *are* you?

CHORUS 1
Foul is fair!

CHORUS 2
Fair is foul!

CHORUS 3
Magazines.

CHORUS 4
Newspapers.

LEADER
We are the public. We own this world.

CHORUS
Together.
We are God, Jack Abbott.

LEADER
What do you think about *that*?

ABBOTT
I think you are crazy!

LEADER
Tauntingly.
You were arrested seventy days later while you worked in the oil fields of Louisiana—and brought back to New York.

ABBOTT
Testily.
There was no argument over a restroom.

LEADER
In surprise.
What? Why has every newspaper and television show been saying that ever since it happened?

ABBOTT
Impatiently.
How should I know? I don't know why the papers say that.

LEADER
What was on his mind?

ABBOTT
I was never able to find out. I don't know what he was thinking. I did something that made him angry. But I do not know what I did to upset him. It was an accident.

LEADER
Didactically, index finger up.
Let's get something perfectly clear: Adan could not have done anything wrong. Whatever happened, Adan was totally innocent.

CHORUS
Laughing among themselves.
Innocent! Innocent!

LEADER
Humorously.
Totally!

ABBOTT
Sarcastically.
Yes, I understand. All the pictures of him in the newspapers were old photographs, taken when he was eighteen years old. The media's the message.

CHORUS
Together, smugly.
Right!

LEADER
Lecturing.
You got the message. Adan was the victim from the beginning! You've already been convicted. You have entered the circle.

ABBOTT
That is why no one in New York will visit me in jail.

LEADER
They are afraid.

CHORUS
Together.
Afraid!

LEADER
Afraid they will be attacked by the Public.

CHORUS
Together.
Afraid!

LEADER
They've thrown you to the dogs.

CHORUS
Together.
Afraid!

LEADER
They pretend to believe everything in the newspapers.

ABBOTT
Then we will all go crazy together! I've learned nothing. None of the witnesses will speak to us. The police have warned them to stay away from us.

LEADER
Waving CHORUS into silence dramatically, she addresses audience.
The Judge calls this court to order. Case on trial continues between the State of New York and Jack Henry Abbott. Defendant is on trial for Second Degree Murder. The Defendant, his Attorney, and the District Attorney are all present. All sides stipulate to the presence of all sworn jurors.

Gavel bangs off-stage.

CHORUS begins to sway, chanting softly in a high-pitched voice:
A time to live, a time to die
No curse can live upon a lie.
(repeated twice)

LEADER
As the CHORUS chants and sways, she shouts in response, throwing up her fist each time:
Da capo! da capo! Again!

Scene 2

As the LEADER shouts, the stage gradually grows dark, except over ABBOTT. The last "da capo!" cues the CHORUS, which fades away at the back of the stage. Right side of the stage lights up with dim (perhaps yellow) lighting—revealing in obscurity a desk and the faceless DEFENSE LAWYER. He delivers his lines, moving around the desk as he speaks, making thespian flourishes. He sits at the

desk, on the desk, paces with his hands behind his back, etc. The
LEADER throws back her head wildly and laughs as she exits.
ABBOTT's stool becomes a witness stand.

DEFENSE LAWYER
Mr. Abbott, how old are you?

ABBOTT
I'm thirty-seven.

DEFENSE LAWYER
Okay. Mr. Abbott, have you been to prison?

ABBOTT
Yes.

DEFENSE LAWYER
How many years were you in prison?

ABBOTT
Adult prison, nineteen years.

DEFENSE LAWYER
Juvenile prison?

ABBOTT
Five years.

DEFENSE LAWYER
From age twelve to the present, Mr. Abbott, how long have you not been
in prison?

ABBOTT
Nine months.

DEFENSE LAWYER
Mr. Abbott, how much formal education have you had?

ABBOTT
You mean in school?

DEFENSE LAWYER
Yes, sir.

ABBOTT
Up to the sixth grade.

DEFENSE LAWYER
Did you finish the sixth grade?

ABBOTT
No.

DEFENSE LAWYER
Were you ever in any prison schools?

ABBOTT
No.

DEFENSE LAWYER
Do you regard yourself as educated now?

ABBOTT
Yes.

DEFENSE LAWYER
How did that happen?

ABBOTT
Well, I've done a lot of things.

DEFENSE LAWYER
Like what?

ABBOTT
Well, I think I've experienced a lot of things and that's—

DEFENSE LAWYER
Did you do much reading?

ABBOTT
Yes.

DEFENSE LAWYER
What area?

ABBOTT
Everything, everything.

DEFENSE LAWYER
Mathematics?

ABBOTT
Yes.

DEFENSE LAWYER
How high did you go in mathematics?

ABBOTT
I don't know.

DEFENSE LAWYER
What's the last thing you studied in mathematics?

ABBOTT
Logic.

DEFENSE LAWYER
Are you familiar with Einstein's theory of relativity?

ABBOTT
Yes.

DEFENSE LAWYER
Do you feel like you know it?

ABBOTT
Yes, some of it, yes.

DEFENSE LAWYER
How about philosophy, sir?

ABBOTT
Yes, I know philosophy.

DEFENSE LAWYER
Whom have you studied?

ABBOTT
All of them.

DEFENSE LAWYER
All of them. Science?

ABBOTT
Yes.

DEFENSE LAWYER
Religion?

ABBOTT
Yes.

DEFENSE LAWYER
History?

ABBOTT
Yes.

DEFENSE LAWYER
Dialectics?

ABBOTT
Yes.

DEFENSE LAWYER
Political Science?

ABBOTT
Yes.

DEFENSE LAWYER
Karl Marx, for example?

ABBOTT
Yes.

DEFENSE LAWYER
You learned a lot from what you could read?

ABBOTT
As I said, from what I've done. Like you said yourself, dialectics. Someone told me the other day that I was dialectical. I understand what he
means.

DEFENSE LAWYER
There came a time when you began to write letters to Norman Mailer. Is
that so?

ABBOTT
Yes.

DEFENSE LAWYER
What was your purpose in writing to Mr. Mailer?

ABBOTT
To make a record. To give him information.

DEFENSE LAWYER
Of what?

ABBOTT
Of all this.

DEFENSE LAWYER
Are you the author of a book called *In the Belly of the Beast*?

ABBOTT
I am. Those weren't the letters though.

DEFENSE LAWYER
What is *In the Belly of the Beast*? What is in that book?

ABBOTT
It's about me.

DEFENSE LAWYER
Who wrote it?

ABBOTT
I wrote it. You know.

DEFENSE LAWYER
Does it come in part from the letters you wrote to Mr. Mailer?

ABBOTT
Yes, but only about a third of the book. I wrote the rest especially for the book. But my parole had nothing to do with the book. My time was over in prison. I had been writing Mailer for several years, as a friend.

DEFENSE LAWYER
You got out. You were placed in the halfway house the beginning of June, and you stopped going there on the morning of July 18th. Is that right?

ABBOTT
Yes.

DEFENSE LAWYER
About six, seven weeks.

ABBOTT
Yes. Six weeks.

DEFENSE LAWYER
Mr. Abbott, between June and July 18th, did there come a time when you met a woman named Veronique de St. André?

ABBOTT
Yes.

DEFENSE LAWYER
About how much time did you spend with Veronique between, I guess, the beginning of June and July 18th?

ABBOTT
Well, she was—she wasn't an American, and I spent as much time as possible, and she was—she was teaching me manners, you know, she was teaching me about music. She had Mozart.

DEFENSE LAWYER
Did there come a time when you met a woman named Susan Roxas?

ABBOTT
Yes.

DEFENSE LAWYER
How did you meet her, Mr. Abbott?

ABBOTT
I met her at Veronique's apartment.

DEFENSE LAWYER
And did you and Susan spend much time together?

ABBOTT
We had just begun to. A little.

DEFENSE LAWYER
Mr. Abbott, I'd like to invite your attention to the week before July 18th, 1981.

ABBOTT
Yes.

DEFENSE LAWYER
Were you aware that your book *In the Belly of the Beast* was going to be reviewed in *The New York Times* "Book Review" section?

ABBOTT
Yeah, I read it.

DEFENSE LAWYER
You read the review?

ABBOTT
Yes.

DEFENSE LAWYER
And when in point of time did you do that?

ABBOTT
I got advance—Random House got advance copies about maybe ten days or two weeks before.

DEFENSE LAWYER
How was the review?

ABBOTT
Well, it was—it was a little effusive, but I don't like this—There is a lot about it I didn't like, but it was, as far as a literary review, it was the best.

DEFENSE LAWYER
Would it be fair to characterize the review as a rave?

ABBOTT
Yes, that's what they say.

DEFENSE LAWYER
Mr. Abbott, did there come a time when you put a knife in the chest of Richard Adan?

ABBOTT
Yes.

DEFENSE LAWYER
Mr. Abbott, I'm going to ask you, first, to tell this jury how it happened as it appeared to you on the night of July 18th and then I'm going to ask you to tell this jury how you now understand it actually happened. Okay?

ABBOTT
Yes.

DEFENSE LAWYER
And I'd like to begin with your meeting with Miss Roxas and Miss de St. André.

ABBOTT
All right. I was—I had returned from work and it was too late—I had returned from work, and it was too late to eat at the halfway house, so I went across the street to a new place that is opening up there. It's a pretty nice place called The Great Jones Café.

The left side of the stage glows to reveal SUSAN and VERONI-QUE. ABBOTT speaks to them from his stool, and they in turn interact. ABBOTT also, at appropriate places, speaks to the DE-FENSE LAWYER.

SUSAN
Speaking to the audience.
I saw Jack sitting at the far end of the restaurant, and he was eating. So I said "Hello," and he came over and joined us.

ABBOTT
To SUSAN and VERONIQUE.
Hello Susan. Veronique.

DEFENSE LAWYER
And after you met Ms. Roxas and Ms. de St. André at the restaurant, how long did you remain there?

ABBOTT
We were there for two or three hours.

SUSAN
To the audience.
Veronique said that we should go dancing.

VERONIQUE
To ABBOTT and SUSAN.
It is an after-hours place, in SoHo. Called the Berliner. Let's go.

SUSAN
To VERONIQUE.
I have heard bad rumors about that place. I do not know.

VERONIQUE
What kind of rumors? What did you hear?

SUSAN
That there was a lot—a lot of potential violence there.

VERONIQUE
Speaking to ABBOTT.
Do you want to go, Jack? What do you think?

ABBOTT
To VERONIQUE.
Well, it's alright with me. I have to go back to the halfway house.
Turns head to DEFENSE LAWYER and continues.
I went back and I put on a pair of Levi's, and I had a knife, a paring knife.

SUSAN
Piping in, brightly.
He tucked it into his pants, and I laughed. I said he might hurt himself first. But it never had a sharp point. It looked like sort of a spatula.

Light to left of the stage goes out. SUSAN and VERONIQUE vanish.

ABBOTT
A kitchen knife.

DEFENSE LAWYER
Where did you get that knife?

ABBOTT
It was laying on the table, my bureau table.

DEFENSE LAWYER
Why did you take that knife with you then, Mr. Abbott?

ABBOTT
Well, the Slasher had just been apprehended about three blocks away, and I witnessed a killing, a stabbing death, on the corner of Fourth Street, Second Avenue. In front of a deli.

DEFENSE LAWYER
In that neighborhood?

ABBOTT
Yeah. And I witnessed three stabbings in front of the men's shelter, and I had been threatened with violence. I had been accosted on the streets. I had money taken away from me on the sidewalks. And—I had only had to carry it on three or four occasions. We were on foot.

DEFENSE LAWYER
What about other people at the halfway house? Did you ever see them with knives?

ABBOTT
The people who work in the halfway house, everyone of them carries a knife.

DEFENSE LAWYER
Mr. Abbott, did you have knives in prison?

ABBOTT
Yes.

DEFENSE LAWYER
Was that a rare occurrence?

ABBOTT
No, you always had to know where there was a weapon.

DEFENSE LAWYER
You always had to have access to a weapon in prison?

ABBOTT
Yes.

DEFENSE LAWYER
Why?

ABBOTT
Because—because they kill each other in prison for nothing.

DEFENSE LAWYER
How did you like the nightclub?

ABBOTT
It was friendly, people were joking, and we were buying drinks, and people were buying us drinks. We left there happy, and Susan and Veronique were kind of joyous. I was feeling good. It was about four in the morning when we walked out.

Light to left of the stage goes on, revealing VERONIQUE.

VERONIQUE
To ABBOTT.
There is a café by your place, Jack. Let's stop for breakfast. It is a clean place.

ABBOTT
To VERONIQUE.
If you want to, it's fine with me.

VERONIQUE
This is it. The Binibon? Do I say it correctly?

ABBOTT
Yes, Binibon.
He turns his head to the DEFENSE LAWYER. VERONIQUE vanishes in darkness.
I knew we shouldn't have been in that neighborhood that late at night, and I knew that I should go back to the halfway house—but—but the girls were hungry, so I said "Okay."

DEFENSE LAWYER
So what happened when you got in there?

ABBOTT
We took the table by the wall, and someone appeared with three menus, and he laid the menus on the table in front of us.

Scene 3

The left of the stage lights up, brightly. The light over ABBOTT and the DEFENSE LAWYER dims. The light reveals SUSAN, the AB-

BOTT CHARACTER, and VERONIQUE seated at a small table. SUSAN sits facing the ABBOTT CHARACTER; VERONIQUE is to his left. ADAN appears and drops menus on the table, in a stack. He then stands there, watching. SUSAN and VERONIQUE pick up menus and open them. The ABBOTT CHARACTER looks up at ADAN, who is standing to his right, facing VERONIQUE. The ABBOTT CHARACTER speaks and enacts the scene, as ABBOTT, to the side, narrates in response to the DEFENSE LAWYER's questions. ADAN speaks as well.

DEFENSE LAWYER
Is that someone you know to be Richard Adan?

ABBOTT
Richard Adan, yes.

ABBOTT CHARACTER speaks after SUSAN and VERONIQUE pick up their menus.

ABBOTT CHARACTER
I'll take bacon and eggs and . . .

ADAN
Bluntly interrupting.
I don't take orders.

SUSAN and VERONIQUE look up from their menus at the ABBOTT CHARACTER, wide-eyed. Then all three look at ADAN, curiously. ADAN simply stands there.

ABBOTT
And I looked at—Susan looked at me, and I looked over at Veronique and they shrugged. We didn't know what to say, and so I said, well, I said—

ABBOTT CHARACTER
Well, who—who *does* take orders? What are we going to do, wait on ourselves? What are you standing there for?

At this point ADAN interrupts again, placing his left hand on the shoulder of the ABBOTT CHARACTER, who is bewildered. ADAN is condescending. SUSAN and VERONIQUE are stunned.

ABBOTT
I tried to pull my shoulder away, but he would not remove his hand. And then he pushed back on my shoulder, and he said—

ADAN pointing with his right hand to a point to his right, somewhere behind SUSAN. He speaks and acts as if he were talking to idiots.

ADAN
See that guy down there?

ABBOTT CHARACTER, SUSAN, and VERONIQUE all crane around to see where he is pointing, embarrassed. ADAN waits until everyone is focused on the WAITER.

ADAN
Lecturing.
That's the guy that takes the orders.
ADAN then removes his hand and steps back, surveying them.

ABBOTT
He removed his hand and stepped back, sort of contemptuously. And so we were relieved, you know. What was an awkward situation was over with. And Adan signaled him and he came over.

The WAITER comes up, from behind SUSAN. He stands behind her. ADAN withdraws.

ABBOTT
I gave him my order.

ABBOTT CHARACTER
I'll have eggs, bacon, and coffee—black.

The WAITER writes on a pad.

ABBOTT
Susan and Veronique had their menus, and they were talking in French. But I leaned back in my chair, and I remember this middle-aged worker was eating and he caught my attention and he—His eyes were looking over at Adan apprehensively, and it drew my attention over further. And I looked and this guy is standing there with his arms folded.

DEFENSE LAWYER
Was this Adan?

ABBOTT
Yes. And he was glaring at me. And he said—

ADAN is standing outside the circle of light over the table, but his voice comes through clearly. It does not sound *obnoxious. It sounds neither cordial nor seriously put, however.*

ADAN
What are you looking at?

ABBOTT CHARACTER abruptly turns his face away from ADAN and enacts the following:

ABBOTT
And so I leaned forward to the table and tried to get involved in the conversation, you know. Then I heard it again.

ADAN
Challengingly.
What are you looking at?

ABBOTT CHARACTER deliberately ignores this.

ABBOTT
I'm thinking this guy is making a scene. He's going to start some trouble right here. And I looked at Susan and Veronique and I thought, oh man, I'm thinking about the halfway house, too. I have to get back there before seven o'clock.*

ADAN
What are you looking at?

---

*Abbott was referring to the fact that it was too late to leave and find another café, since it would be too time-consuming for them to walk uptown and randomly look for another café at that hour. Taxis did not stop in that neighborhood.

SUSAN and VERONIQUE do not notice. They are talking about the menus.

ABBOTT
And I heard it again, and I said—

ABBOTT CHARACTER turns his face toward ADAN'S voice. His tone is incredulous.

ABBOTT CHARACTER
Wh-what!? What!?

Lights go out, and props and actors vanish. The focus passes to ABBOTT while he delivers these lines:

ABBOTT
I looked directly at him to let him know he couldn't just start in on me. It would just be a short period before he was over at the table and trying something. So I excused myself from the table, and I stepped over to him. I'm thinking: What is the matter with him? Did I do something wrong?

Scene 4

The lighting goes on again where the last scene took place, the table now empty. ADAN is standing, with hands on hips, aggressively. The ABBOTT CHARACTER appears and approaches ADAN.

ABBOTT
I noted his appearance. His hair was short and combed straight back like a convict. He had on a black t-shirt and he was muscular. He looked like he could—was physical. I took him for about twenty-six years old.

CHORUS LEADER
She pipes in loudly, off-stage.
The State testified Adan was five feet, seven inches tall and weighed one-hundred-and-forty-five pounds. That was a lie. He was five feet, nine inches tall. He weighed one-hundred-and-seventy pounds. He outweighed Abbott by almost fifty pounds.

ABBOTT CHARACTER
Politely.
What's bothering you? Have I done something to you?

ADAN
Harshly.
Nothing's bothering *me*. What's bothering *you*?

ABBOTT CHARACTER
Why did you say that to me?

ADAN
Loudly.
Say what!?

ABBOTT
He glared at me. I saw a snarl on his face. I started to walk back to the table.

ABBOTT CHARACTER turns away to return to the table.

ABBOTT
And he made another remark.

ADAN
To the back of the ABBOTT CHARACTER.
I said, what are you looking at!?

ABBOTT CHARACTER spins back around, facing ADAN.

ABBOTT
So I turned back to him and I said—

ABBOTT CHARACTER
Insultingly.
Listen, pal! You're making a scene! Now if I've done something to bother you, *spit* it out! So we can correct it!

ADAN'S eyes narrow; he stiffens.

ABBOTT CHARACTER
Irritated.
If I've done something wrong, *tell me.* But do so in a lower tone of voice because everyone is looking. It's not necessary! I'm not going to argue in the middle of this floor.

ABBOTT
I'm thinking if there is something genuinely wrong, it can be ironed out. Because I never came there to start trouble.

ADAN
Threateningly.
Do you want to leave? Do you want to go outside?

ABBOTT CHARACTER is stunned at this. He takes it as a threat—a challenge to fight.

ADAN
Pushing it.
Do you want me to put you out the door?!

ABBOTT CHARACTER
Confused.
You don't have to tell me what to do!

At this moment the WAITER is coming up behind the ABBOTT CHARACTER, carrying dishes. As he does this, the ABBOTT CHARACTER glances to his left and stops the WAITER as the WAITER comes around. He blocks the WAITER's path with his left arm. The WAITER stops, confused. ADAN spins on his heel abruptly and walks to a shelf behind the counter, three steps away. ADAN is moving quickly. The ABBOTT CHARACTER keeps his eyes on ADAN as he speaks. ADAN walks quickly to a shelf, picks up a knife with his right hand, puts it in his right pocket (under his short change-pouch), keeps both hands in his pocket (holding the weapon), and strides back up to the ABBOTT CHARACTER. As this action takes place, the ABBOTT CHARACTER speaks to the WAITER.

ABBOTT CHARACTER
Urgently.
What's wrong with him?!

WAITER
Vaguely.
Don't pay attention to him.

*The WAITER moves on just as ADAN (returning) is a step away
from the ABBOTT CHARACTER. ADAN walks up and hits the
ABBOTT CHARACTER deliberately with his chest (against the
ABBOTT CHARACTER's chest). The ABBOTT CHARACTER
steps back, surprised.*

ABBOTT CHARACTER
Loudly.
You don't have to push me! I'll go outside, but only to talk. I've got no
quarrel with you.

*ABBOTT CHARACTER lifts up front of his shirt, exposing the
handle of his paring knife. ADAN looks at it, unmoved.*

ABBOTT CHARACTER
I've got a knife myself, but I don't want any trouble.

ADAN
Pointing at the door.
Get going! Let's go!

*ABBOTT CHARACTER glances once over at SUSAN and VE-
RONIQUE and starts, reluctantly, toward the door. ADAN walks
briskly in front of him as he follows. Lights go out again and focus
shifts to ABBOTT, as he delivers the following lines:*

ABBOTT
I'm thinking, now, whenever he first told me to step outside, I paused and
looked at him. I took him to be something different than what he was. I
looked at him and I thought, well, he's—full of shit. He's not going to do
anything to me. He's just bluffing.

The light goes on again. There is a prop door ADAN is holding open with his left hand, his right still concealed. He stands on the sidewalk, since the door opens outward. The ABBOTT CHARACTER steps out the door and turns toward ADAN. At that moment, a customer is entering the café, and he pauses because the ABBOTT CHARACTER is blocking the way.

ADAN
Harshly.
Get out of the way!

The ABBOTT CHARACTER steps backwards, and the customer enters. He starts to speak to ADAN, as the customer goes past. ADAN releases the door and steps toward him.

ADAN
Keep going!

The ABBOTT CHARACTER turns and takes a step or two down the sidewalk and pauses. He starts to turn around, and ADAN walks toward him, shooing him with his left hand.

ADAN
Let's go! Get going! I said keep moving!

The ABBOTT CHARACTER is confused. He obeys. He turns and keeps walking two or three steps to the corner. Then he turns around one more time to speak to ADAN, but ADAN steps quickly toward him again.

ADAN
Keep going!

The ABBOTT CHARACTER is dazed now. He turns the corner. The distance the ABBOTT CHARACTER has covered, from door to the corner, is only five steps.

ABBOTT
I'm thinking, this can't be—he's not that foolish, you know. And so I walked, and he's walking behind me. At one point he is not saying anything to me. But as I turned the corner, it's like entering a dark alley.

Note: The lighting on Second Avenue is glaring, very bright. It is the coming out of this light that makes Fifth Street appear so dark, so suddenly.

ABBOTT
It frightened me. I stopped and turned around, and I could see him standing there. And he had his hand in his pocket. He glanced up and down Second Avenue.

The ABBOTT CHARACTER begins to take a tentative step back toward Second Avenue; ADAN is facing him, standing on the corner.

ABBOTT
I'm thinking, I can't let this go any further. I shouted at him.

The ABBOTT CHARACTER withdraws his knife and brandishes it so ADAN can see it.

ABBOTT CHARACTER
Shouting.
I can hear you from there! You tell me what's wrong! Don't come any closer to me! Stay back!

ADAN looks at the ABBOTT CHARACTER brandishing the knife. ADAN's eyes are probably blinded, too, looking into the darker Fifth Street.

DEFENSE LAWYER
Verbally you were telling him this?

ABBOTT
I was *shouting* at him, and he came right at me, and he pulled out his knife and swung it at me.

ADAN gives the ABBOTT CHARACTER a final "bum's rush," to move him along. ADAN pounces one step, withdraws his knife with his right hand, then starts on a second step. When he takes his first step, the ABBOTT CHARACTER steps at him also, and ADAN never completes his second step. He and the ABBOTT CHAR-

ACTER collide. The ABBOTT CHARACTER, when ADAN starts toward him, rushes forward and clutches ADAN's forearm at the same time he swings his knife. The ABBOTT CHARACTER crouches low and leans to the side as they collide, clutching ADAN's forearm with his left hand.

ABBOTT
I thought I only slashed him across the chest, and then suddenly his hand dropped.

The ABBOTT CHARACTER releases ADAN's arm. ADAN has stopped, in a stiff upright position—totally rigid.

ABBOTT
The knife was in him, and he was dead still. His hands were to his sides.

ABBOTT CHARACTER
He pulls back the knife and steps back, facing ADAN, and says, screaming:
Okay, you! Do you want some more trouble? Do you?!

ABBOTT
And then he brought his hands up to his chest, and that's when I saw there was nothing in his hand, and I looked at the sidewalk and nothing was there.

The ABBOTT CHARACTER, still alert to the possibility that it was a trick, glances at the sidewalk. Debris from the garbage bags is everywhere.

ADAN
His hands over his chest.
You didn't have to kill me.

The ABBOTT CHARACTER, confused, steps toward him.

ABBOTT
I stepped toward him and started to touch him, but I couldn't. I reached for him, and he started walking backward.

DEFENSE LAWYER
Backpedalling?

ADAN and the ABBOTT CHARACTER enact the following action.

ABBOTT
He started walking backwards, and I started to touch him, but I couldn't touch him. I'm looking at his face. He looks like he's dead and there are a lot of strange noises coming up out of his respiratory system, out of his— through his throat. And I'm walking and I am thinking, I have to get—I have to get the girls out of there. I didn't want to be associated with this thing. I thought he would collapse before he got to Second Avenue. That's when I noticed I had entered the window, the side window where people inside the café could look out and see me. That's when I stepped back and got my bearings and put the knife away, under my shirt. He continued.

DEFENSE LAWYER
Onto Second Avenue?

ABBOTT
Yes. Now there was a man—

Pedestrian passes between ADAN and the ABBOTT CHARAC-TER, as ADAN steps backwards onto Second Avenue. He glances once at ADAN and then stares directly at the ABBOTT CHAR-ACTER as he passes. There are many pedestrians on the sidewalk. He passes about four feet in front of the ABBOTT CHARACTER.*

ABBOTT
He was crossing Fifth Street and passed between Adan and I. Adan was walking directly toward the traffic. I was imagining seeing him hit. So I shouted at the pedestrians.

ABBOTT CHARACTER
Shouting.
Stop him! The fool is drunk, and he's walking into the traffic! He doesn't know what he is doing! Stop him! Stop him!

---

*Cf. Appendix I, Section 2, B.

ABBOTT

I was coming onto Second Avenue when I was shouting this, looking like everyone else.

Lights go out; actors and scene vanish. Light focuses on ABBOTT. The rest of the lines (except ABBOTT's and DEFENSE LAW-YER's) are delivered by actors in semi-darkness on the left of the stage; they appear and disappear, in turn, with the lighting.

ABBOTT

With mounting awe.

And at the last moment, about three feet from the curb, he did a—he did a perfect right angle turn and started walking up Second Avenue. Still walking backward. I was—I was stunned. The whole thing was so macabre I couldn't grasp— Then Adan stopped dead. Then he dropped to his knees in a perfect—and then his arms dropped directly to his sides. There was a moment, and then he went directly onto his face. And so, I—like I said, gathered my senses, my senses together and—I—take a few steps towards him and I look. There's a river of blood coming out from under his body at a high velocity. I saw the blood, and I stepped back and I walked over to the café. I didn't want to get everybody's attention. So I stepped in there and I caught the attention of Susan, first, and she saw me and she waved and I signaled her. She tapped Veronique, and they started becoming serious, and they both looked at me. And I said, "Come on, let's go." And so they got up, concerned.

VERONIQUE and SUSAN appear to the left, out of darkness.

SUSAN

To ABBOTT.

What happened?

ABBOTT

To SUSAN.

I think I killed him.

SUSAN

Why?

ABBOTT

I'll tell you later.

SUSAN and VERONIQUE
Run, Jack. Run!

The women vanish in darkness.

DEFENSE LAWYER
Did you intend to kill him?

ABBOTT
No.

A horn sounds.

DEFENSE LAWYER
Excuse me, Mr. Abbott. You just told us how this thing appeared to you at the time. Tell us what you now think happened.

ABBOTT
Confused.
Yesterday Mr. Burdes, a waiter from the deli across the street, mentioned that male customers at the café are told to go outside and around the corner to urinate on the sidewalk by the dumpsters on the curb of Fifth Street.* When I heard that I started thinking and my first impression was that he was manufacturing obvious lies. It was the first time I had ever heard such a thing. It was never mentioned in the media. If you recall, I was going to dismiss you as my lawyer that day and you had told me to think it over. I did not think you had properly brought out enough of Susan's testimony and not enough of Mr. Majesky's and the different people that are involved.

You told me to reconsider dismissing you, and that night, in my cell, it occurred to me that I had not made any inferences previously from the café to Fifth Street except that he took me back there to assault me, and there was no connection between the café and Fifth Street. But the Deli waiter made the connection when he testified that Binibon customers urinate on Fifth Street. I can take it from the beginning and reinterpret what happened. It is the only other way I could account for what was in the back of Adan's mind. I took him to be a hoodlum.

---

*Cf. Appendix II, Section 3.

ABBOTT looks around vaguely and begins to gesticulate as he speaks. He adjusts his glasses. He is in another world. His tone changes.

Norman got me in to see the rehearsal of his play. Plays have been on my mind because it forces me to think in more external terms. In writing novels I become too subjective, too engrossed in detail. So that is why I went to the rehearsal. I was taking notes and studying the actors. I was asking questions and held discussions with actors. I was fascinated by how a play comes from the manuscript onto the stage. That is why Adan would have been a fine actor. Someone told me that this feeling that a good actor has is self-centeredness, which makes them feel proud, and you could mistake it for arrogance. . . .*

CHORUS LEADER walks on stage holding arms over head, CHORUS 1 following.

LEADER
Interferes loudly.
All right! Enough of that! And so Abbott speculated on an interpretation of all of Adan's actions that was not true. He stipulated this was the only alternative: That he either acted in self-defense or was emotionally disturbed if Adan in fact was showing him where to urinate. After he did this, the Prosecutor stipulated to the court—

CHORUS 1
Loudly.
The Prosecutor said: "Your Honor, I want to stipulate here for the record that it was not my intention that Mr. Burdes make statements about any suggestion that Adan was taking Abbott outside to show him where to urinate. Mr. Burdes should not have said that.

---

*Abbott went on for what made up twenty or thirty pages in the trial transcript re-interpreting his memory of the events. His memory was exactly the same. He only interpreted everything from Adan's point of view given the abstract theory that Adan was only trying to help him and only appeared to be angry. By any legal standard Abbott was incompetent when he testified to these speculations. It was clear from interviews with the jurors that Abbott's attempt to justify Adan demonstrated that Abbott's account of how it appeared to him that night was in fact true.

LEADER
Gravely.
So stipulated.

CHORUS 1 lingers. Light shines on the left of the stage. LT. MAJESKY
appears sitting on a stool. ABBOTT listens while the LEADER addresses
the actor.

LEADER
Please state your name and form of employment.

LT. MAJESKY
My name is Lieutenant William Majesky. I am a detective for the New
York Police Department, Ninth Precinct, homicide division.*

LEADER
Are you in charge of the investigation of the Abbott case?

LT. MAJESKY
I am.

LEADER
And you are assisting the Prosecutor in this trial, at this moment, are you
not?

LT. MAJESKY
Yes, that is why I sit beside him at his table during this trial. I advise him.
Give him information.

LEADER
Is it your position or the Prosecutor's position that Adan was showing
Abbott where to urinate when he went outside with Abbott?

LT. MAJESKY
Of course not. It was merely a theory made up by Mr. Burdes, the kid
who works at the deli across the street. He invented that theory. The
urination story is garbage. It's not true.

---

*Cf. Appendix II, Section 1.

LEADER
Why do you think Adan went outside with Abbott?

LT. MAJESKY
My feeling is that Adan went outside with Abbott to calm him down.

LEADER
The State is contending Adan went outside to calm Abbott down?

LT. MAJESKY
Yes. The urination story is garbage.*

LEADER
To calm him down. To calm Abbott down. Why?

CHORUS 1
Shouting.
Abbott went outside to calm *Adan* down, and they all know it. They know Adan kicked Abbott out of the café, but their only concern is to convict Abbott and send him back to prison.
She exits, running.

A cello plays.

---

*Cf. Appendix III, Section 2.

ACT III

Only, that it is necessary with such a desire to be clear what spectacle one will see in any case: Merely an epilogue farce, merely the continued proof that the long, real tragedy is at an end, assuming that every philosophy was in its genesis a long tragedy.

Jenseits von Gut und Böse, No. 25
—Nietzsche

Epilogue

ABBOTT is seated on a stool in the center. To the right of the stage is a desk, as in Act II. This act is a simple farce. Instructions for props are unnecessary. The effects are all done with light and music.

A horn sounds. A banner is brought on stage, reading "The Case Against Abbott." Lights go up on stage. The LEADER sits in a chair behind the desk. The PROSECUTOR walks on stage from the left side, stops in front of ABBOTT, and addresses the audience. The actor should deliver the lines so that the understanding is crystal clear, as if it were a speech or a lecture. ABBOTT watches silently.

PROSECUTOR
Intelligently.
I am the Prosecutor who tried Abbott. What you have so far seen enacted before your senses is an accurate portrayal of the relevant parts of Abbott's trial. The parts that have been left out of this play are the emotional parts of the testimony of one man, Mr. Larsen.

Also left out of this play are the prison reports I read to Mr. Abbott when he was on trial. Out of a prison record covering almost nineteen years, I could only find two reports against Abbott which even suggested he had violent conflicts with other inmates. One of them was an informant report, where an inmate asked to be protected because he was afraid of Abbott. This report was unknown to Abbott. The other report I read to Abbott turned out to be a report that Abbott had requested an FBI investigation of the death of an inmate in a jail, whom the guards said committed suicide. Both these reports were over ten years old. All the other reports of violence in Abbott's record were reports of violence against guards.

Naturally, I did not read these reports because they would have made Abbott appear in a good light, since all these reports portray Abbott beating up prison guards single-handedly five and six at a time. He even beat up nine armed guards once in Marion Prison. So I never read these reports, which were all lies to justify the guards beating up Abbott.

When Abbott was on the witness stand, I did not ask him questions about the crime he was on trial for. I asked him only one question: "You did not think Adan had a knife, did you?" That was the only question I asked him about the crime he was on trial for. I spent one whole day reading prison reports and the next day reading passages out of his book about prison.

So please do not get the impression this play is one-sided and that it has neglected to portray the Prosecutor's case against Abbott. Everyone in this play, except Abbott, was a prosecution witness.

The PROSECUTOR steps away from in front of ABBOTT and strides over to the desk. He sits on the desk-top. The lighting goes out on the left side of the stage again. The PROSECUTOR continues. He holds a clipboard that he reads from when he starts his "cross-examination." He looks at the audience.

These were the only questions I asked Abbott on the last day of my cross-examination. I read select parts of the book on prison he wrote, after reading the nonsense from his prison record the day before. This is my case against him.

He looks at ABBOTT.

LEADER rises, and CHORUS 1 enters. LEADER announces:

LEADER
Case on trial is continued between the State of New York and Jack Henry Abbott. The Defendant, his attorney, the District Attorney, and all sworn jurors are present.

PROSECUTOR
He changes his attitude; his voice is hard, embittered.
Answer the questions, yes or no. Did you write this? THIS THING RE-LATED ABOUT EMOTIONS IS THE HIDDEN, DARK SIDE OF STATE-RAISED CONVICTS. THE FOUL UNDERBELLY EVERYONE HIDES FROM EVERYONE

ELSE. THERE IS SOMETHING ELSE. IT IS THE OTHER HALF, WHICH CON-
CERNS JUDGMENT, REASON, MORAL AND ETHICAL CULTURE. IT IS THE
MANTLE OF PRIDE, INTEGRITY, HONOR. IT IS THE HIGH ESTEEM WE
NATURALLY HAVE FOR VIOLENCE, FORCE. IT IS WHAT MAKES US EF-
FECTIVE MEN WHOSE JUDGMENT IMPINGES ON OTHERS, THE WORLD.
DANGEROUS KILLERS WHO ACT WITH CALCULATION AND PRINCIPLES,
TO AVENGE THEMSELVES, ESTABLISH AND DEFEND THEIR PRINCIPLES
WITH ACTS OF MURDER. Did you write that, Mr. Abbott?

ABBOTT
Yes.

PROSECUTOR
Did you also write this? THE ONLY THING A CONVICT RESPECTS IN
ANOTHER IS MORAL STRENGTH. THAT IS ALL IT TAKES TO KILL A MAN.
Did you write that, Mr. Abbott?

ABBOTT
Yes.

PROSECUTOR
Did you also write this, Mr. Abbott? HAVE YOU EVER SEEN A MAN
DESPAIR BECAUSE HE CANNOT BRING HIMSELF TO MURDER? I AM NOT
TALKING ABOUT MURDER IN THE HEAT OF COMBAT. I AM SPEAKING OF
COLD-BLOODED, PREMEDITATED MURDER. THE ONLY PRISONERS I
HAVE SEEN WHO DO NOT DESPAIR OF BEING INCAPABLE OF MURDER
ARE THOSE WHO ARE CAPABLE OF IT. MOST OF THEM FIND, SOME-
WHERE DOWN THE LINE, THAT THEY ARE CAPABLE OF IT. TO DISCOVER
THERE WAS NO BASIS FOR YOUR ANXIETIES ABOUT MURDER IS A FEEL-
ING SIMILAR TO THAT OF A YOUNG MAN WHO HAS DOUBTS ABOUT
BEING ABLE TO CONSUMMATE HIS FIRST SEXUAL ENCOUNTER WITH A
WOMAN AND WHEN THE TIME COMES, IF HE DID NOT PERFORM MAG-
NIFICENTLY, AT LEAST HE GOT THE JOB DONE. YOU FEEL STRONGER.
Did you write that, Mr. Abbott?

ABBOTT
Yes.

PROSECUTOR
Did you write this, Mr. Abbott? HERE IN PRISON THE MOST RESPECTED

AMONG US ARE THOSE WHO HAVE KILLED OTHER MEN, PARTICULARLY OTHER PRISONERS. BENEATH ALL RELATIONSHIPS IN PRISON IS THE EVER-PRESENT FACT OF MURDER. IT ULTIMATELY DEFINES OUR RE-LATIONSHIP AMONG OURSELVES. Did you write that, Mr. Abbott?

ABBOTT
Yes.

PROSECUTOR
When you stepped outside with Adan, you didn't think he had a knife, did you? *Did you?*

ABBOTT
I was not absolutely certain, no. But he did have a knife.

PROSECUTOR
Did you write this in your book, Mr. Abbott? WHEN YOU ARE RAGING INSIDE AT ANYONE, YOU LEARN TO CONCEAL IT, TO SMILE OR FEIGN COWARDICE. YOU HAVE TO MOVE INTO TOTAL ACTIVITY FROM A TOTAL-LY INACTIVE POSTURE TO SINK A KNIFE IN AS CLOSE TO HIS HEART AS POSSIBLE. IT IS ALSO THIS THAT UNSETTLES A MAN'S MIND IN PRISON. A KNIFE IS AN INTIMATE WEAPON. VERY PERSONAL. IT UNSETTLES THE MIND BECAUSE YOU ARE NOT KILLING IN PHYSICAL SELF-DEFENSE. YOU ARE KILLING SOMEONE IN ORDER TO LIVE RESPECTABLY IN PRISON. MORAL SELF-DEFENSE. LET'S SAY SOMEONE STEALS SOMETHING FROM YOU. YOU CATCH HIM DOING IT. HE GETS LOUD AND AGGRESSIVE WITH YOU. WHAT YOU MUST DO NEXT IS TO BECOME FRIENDLY WITH HIM. IN PRISON SOCIETY YOU ARE EXPECTED TO PUT A KNIFE IN HIM. SO YOU DISARM HIM WITH FRIENDLINESS TO GET HIM ASIDE AND KILL HIM.

*Two actors appear at the left of the stage out of the dark. They enact the reading.**

PROSECUTOR
HERE IS HOW IT IS: YOU ARE BOTH ALONE IN HIS CELL. YOU'VE SLIPPED OUT A KNIFE. YOU'RE HOLDING IT BESIDE YOUR LEG SO HE CAN'T SEE IT. THE ENEMY IS CHATTERING AWAY ABOUT SOMETHING. YOU SEE HIS

---

*See "Note on the Killer Vignette," Appendix III, Section 3.

EYES. HE THINKS YOU ARE HIS FOOL. YOU SEE THE SPOT. IT'S A TARGET BETWEEN THE SECOND AND THIRD BUTTON ON HIS SHIRT. AS YOU CALMLY TALK AND SMILE, YOU MOVE YOUR LEFT FOOT TO THE SIDE, TO STEP ACROSS HIS RIGHT-SIDE BODY LENGTH. A LIGHT PIVOT TO-WARD HIM WITH YOUR RIGHT SHOULDER AND THE WORLD TURNS UP-SIDE DOWN. YOU HAVE SUNK THE KNIFE INTO THE MIDDLE OF HIS CHEST. SLOWLY HE BEGINS TO STRUGGLE FOR HIS LIFE. AS HE SINKS, YOU HAVE TO KILL HIM FAST OR GET CAUGHT. HE WILL SAY "WHY?" OR "NO!" NOTHING ELSE. YOU CAN FEEL HIS LIFE TREMBLING THROUGH THE KNIFE IN YOUR HAND. IT ALMOST OVERCOMES YOU, THE GENTLE-NESS OF THE FEELING AT THE CENTER OF A COARSE ACT OF MURDER. YOU'VE PUMPED THE KNIFE IN SEVERAL TIMES WITHOUT EVEN BEING AWARE OF IT. YOU GO TO THE FLOOR WITH HIM TO FINISH HIM. IT IS LIKE CUTTING HOT BUTTER, NO RESISTANCE AT ALL. Did you write that, Mr. Abbott? Did you? Did you?

ABBOTT
It's good, isn't it? If it was written by the kind of man who would do such a thing, it would not move you, would it? You wouldn't understand it, and it wouldn't upset you, would it? It is the point of view of an observer.

PROSECUTOR
Very vivid, Mr. Abbott. Did you write it?

ABBOTT
Yes. It portrayed a prisoner stabbed in his cell a great number of times. Not just once.

The PROSECUTOR walks over to the left side of the stage. The LEADER walks around the desk, staying on the right side of the stage. They face the audience, with ABBOTT between them and behind them. These are their closing addresses to the Jury. They deliver them to the audience.

LEADER
Officiously.
Case on trial is continued between the State of New York and Jack Henry Abbott. Closing address to the Jury.

PROSECUTOR

Ladies and gentlemen of the Jury, Mr. Abbott is charged with murdering Richard Adan. The issue is not how he was treated in prison. The issue here is how did the Defendant stab and kill Richard Adan. Was it with intent to kill him, or was it as the Defendant said, without intent to kill?

LEADER

Ladies and gentlemen, Mr. Abbott has not raised any issue of how he was treated in prison. The Prosecutor has done that. The issue here is merely intent to kill. Adan was stabbed only one time. He was stabbed in the breastbone, in the exact center of the chest. The wound was one inch wide, the width of the knife. One inch. The wound was three-and-a-half inches deep. The wound was one inch wide at the surface and tapered to less than a quarter of an inch inside. Adan was seen walking at least thirty or forty yards. And Abbott was seen walking with him. Had Abbott intended to kill Adan, he surely would have stabbed him repeatedly.

Now whether or not Abbott reached around Adan to plant the knife exactly in the center of his chest, with knowledge of killing people, merely has inflammatory value. It is only slander. However Adan was stabbed, he was only stabbed once. Abbott stabbed him from the front as Adan rushed him. How is intent to kill better established by saying he stabbed him from a story he wrote in a book?

Abbott is not saying he did not intend to *harm* Adan.

Abbott nowhere in his book described anyone being stabbed except face-to-face. But the Prosecutor has made the whole issue Abbott's writing ability. Abbott has been tried for writing a book. His book has been used as evidence against him. But Abbott and his book are two different things. Abbott's ability with a pen should not be taken as ability to kill.

PROSECUTOR

Abbott's book demonstrates his personal philosophy. That is all that counts. He believes in murdering people. He writes about it in his book. He set himself up as an expert on violence. Now he should pay for it.

LEADER

Among other things, the Prosecutor has read to the Jury a single passage three times from Mr. Abbott's book, where the situation of a prisoner murdered in his cell is described. On one of his readings, a female juror was so confused that she covered her face with her hands and cried, "Please! Stop it, stop it!" It was a powerful piece of fiction. The Prosecutor is contending that this vignette demonstrates a special knowledge of killing. But it takes no expert to know you can kill a man by stabbing him repeatedly in his chest. A literary vignette should not be a crime. Abbott does not have to stoop to defending his writings. He does not and has never believed in "killing people."

The lights go out, and the PROSECUTOR vanishes in the darkness. The lights come on again and the Jurors (BLUNT and LUCAS) appear in their places. The lighting can be dramatic. They respond to the voice of the LEADER. A cello plays.

LEADER
Officiously.
Case continues. State of New York against Jack Henry Abbott. The Jury is deliberating. Mr. Blunt, were you a member of the Jury that convicted Jack Henry Abbott of manslaughter?

BLUNT
Bewildered.
Yes, I was. I convicted Jack Abbott because I thought he had been convicted of murder before.

LEADER
Mr. Lucas, were you a member of the Jury that convicted Mr. Abbott of manslaughter?

LUCAS
Yes, I was. We were given a sheet with the choices of whether it was murder or manslaughter and the degrees of manslaughter. But there was no choice on that list indicating he might be innocent through self-defense or just not guilty. It wasn't fair. Abbott testified that he acted in self-defense. Most of the other jurors rushed home every night to watch the news and read the newspapers. And after it was over, I read several of the newspapers that covered the trial. Nothing was accurate. The newspapers were saying Abbott had been convicted of killing people before. But that was not brought out at the trial.

LEADER
Accusingly.
The Jury was never sequestered during the trial?

LUCAS
No, ma'am. But we were told not to read his book and not to read newspapers or listen to broadcasts about the case.

After the trial we were sequestered, though. But we could have had a mistrial anytime. I mean people went into the hotel and smuggled radios and papers into the hotel. Things they weren't supposed to have. One woman told us that Adan isn't the first man Jack Abbott killed. She got that out of the newspapers. They were raising things against Abbott in the jury room that were never said in court.

Like this one guy, even before the trial was over, he made statements that Abbott was guilty. I thought it was totally unfair. Everyone wanted to go home. If I had just gone along with the crowd, it would have been over in ten minutes. But I wasn't going to convict him of intent to kill. I would have stayed there six months.

CHORUS 1
Mockingly.
I don't want to spend another night in this fleabag hotel. It's been two days. Let's compromise and vote manslaughter one and get out of here. Anything to put that bastard back in prison.

LUCAS
When I went back into court and had to say "guilty," it really bothered me. I remember choking in my throat. I almost cried. After it was over I got up and walked over to Jack Abbott. I looked him in the face and wished him a happy birthday. To be kind. It was his birthday. And this fat woman, the one who had read his book, she said it in a loud, sarcastic way.

CHORUS 2
She runs across the stage, cutting capers and shouting mockingly.
Yeah! Happy birthday, Jack Abbott!

LUCAS
He didn't say anything. I couldn't expect him to thank me or anything like that. I just wanted him to know I knew it was his birthday. I just wanted to wish him a happy birthday from my heart. But then—

CHORUS 1
Shouting mockingly.
Yeah! Happy birthday, Jack Abbott! HAPPY BIRTHDAY!

*A horn sounds. The lights go out again, and the JURORS vanish.
ABBOTT is alone on stage with the LEADER and CHORUS 1.*

LEADER
Loudly.
Case continues between the State of New York and Jack Henry Abbott.
Is there anything you wish to say before sentence is imposed for man-
slaughter?

ABBOTT
No.

The LEADER draws herself up and produces a large sheet of paper.

LEADER
Resoundingly.
Abbott's judge said this to him:
She then proceeds to read from the paper.
The jury has acquitted the defendant of Murder. The defendant is not
guilty of Murder. The sentence for conviction of first-degree manslaughter
does not exceed six years in the State of New York. However, it is
perfectly clear that the Defendant carried from prison some sort of a
unique philosophy that the smallest slight must be met with the most
violent response. I recall reading a letter by his friend, Professor Malaquais, and he stated that Abbott never read fiction. Perhaps if he had read
fiction he would have been more able to cope with reality. There is no
question of the Defendant's inordinate intelligence; there is no question of
the fact he educated himself to an extraordinary degree. I recall a similar
case involving a man Mr. Abbott's age. He was an extremely gifted
graphic artist. In prison he was offered a job by the head of a pharmaceutical company who was involved in one of these right-wing minority
political groups and had once been in jail for it. But the parole authorities
would not permit him to take this job with the multi-million-dollar
pharmaceutical company because he would have been associating with
criminals. No exception was made for him. Abbott is a repeat offender.
His last conviction was ten years ago during a prison escape and, before
that, twenty years ago. I see no reason not to sentence him as such. The
defendant is sentenced to life imprisonment, for the minimum of fifteen
years before he is considered for parole.

A horn sounds.

CHORUS 1
Mockingly.
The judge is equating Norman Mailer with the man who heads the pharmaceutical company! He is equating Abbott with the graphic artist! Mailer was once convicted for stabbing his wife in the chest four times!—But he did not go to jail for it! Ha! Ha!

Glaring blue light exposes an abstract of a prison cell, on the left of stage. ABBOTT leaves the stool and enters it. ABBOTT sits on the floor beside his bed, picks up a pen, and begins writing, using his bed as a table. The lights begin to dim. The right of stage is lit with yellow lighting. The LEADER stands close to foot of stage-right, facing audience. The LEADER and CHORUS 1 are joined by the rest of the CHORUS. The CHORUS forms a half-circle behind the LEADER, facing the audience. A flute song plays.

Closing Chorus

CHORUS 1
Norman Mailer.

CHORUS 2
Mimicking.
Is Jack Abbott the original seed of evil? Should such a question be raised in a democratic society?

CHORUS 3
Norman Mailer's wife.

CHORUS 4
Mimicking.
I almost divorced Norman for not attacking Abbott.

CHORUS 1
Mailer's friend, José Torres, the boxer and writer for Puerto Rican rights.

CHORUS 2
Mimicking.
The Hispanic community is angry. Adan was a Cuban. They hate Abbott.

CHORUS 3
Erroll McDonald, Abbott's editor, a black man from Costa Rica, educated at Yale University.

CHORUS 4
Mimicking.
Jack Abbott is a racist. He hates blacks. He hates American Indians.

CHORUS 1
The black *60 Minutes* television journalist, Ed Bradley.

CHORUS 2
Mimicking.
You wrote in your book: A WARDEN, A PRESIDENT NIXON, A HITLER WILL NEVER BE ONE OF US. WE COULD NEVER LIVE SIDE BY SIDE WITH THEM THE DAY AFTER THE REVOLUTION. THEY MUST PAY. You said they must pay. Now, what do you think we ought to do to you? What should you pay?*

The lighting on the right of stage, which grew dimmer as these exchanges occurred, goes completely out. Out of the darkness, a light moves from red to purple and blue and gray, fading to blackness again during this reading and as ABBOTT writes. A violin begins to weep. The CHORUS sways rhythmically and vocalizes solemn, ghostly sounds in accompaniment to the reading.

LEADER
With mock sentimentality.
"I would mosey alone out to the main yard, and those were the best moments of my life in prison. Indeed, maybe among the best of spiritual experiences I have known. The worst of the heat of the day would snuggle into the rich, moist ground and a quietude we all respected filled the yard. At most you could detect only a few inmates on the yard but they were always distant, slowly moving figures. When dusk would begin to lower and bloom in gray and purple hues, giving a thick texture to the heavens, it brought the sky down so close it seemed to graze the earth and absorb me in its folds. I remember being wrapped in the fragrant, warm bouquets

---

*Cf. Appendix III, Note 1.

of magnolia and peach blossom and the wet essence of lilac saturating the air as the evening slowly settled across the wide prison yard. I felt *clean,* like a babe again. I never knew evenings like that existed, evenings that do not smell of rusted steel and feel like grainy dust; evenings that irritate your eyes, as if they were dry and tired."

The LEADER and CHORUS bow. Lights snap off.*

CURTAIN

Incipit tragoedia

---

*See Appendix IV for further discussion.

PART TWO

Appendix

APPENDIX I
Diagrams of the Scene and Action

Appendix I, Section 1, A

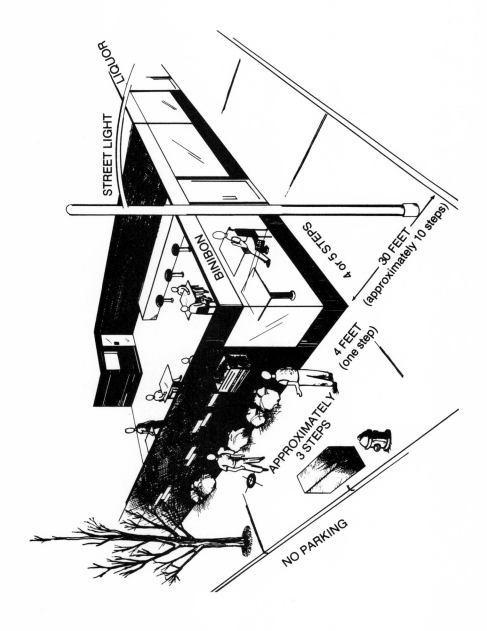

Appendix I, Section 1, B

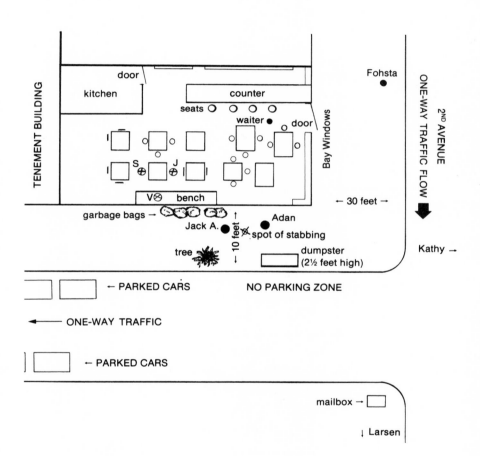

Appendix I, Section 1, C

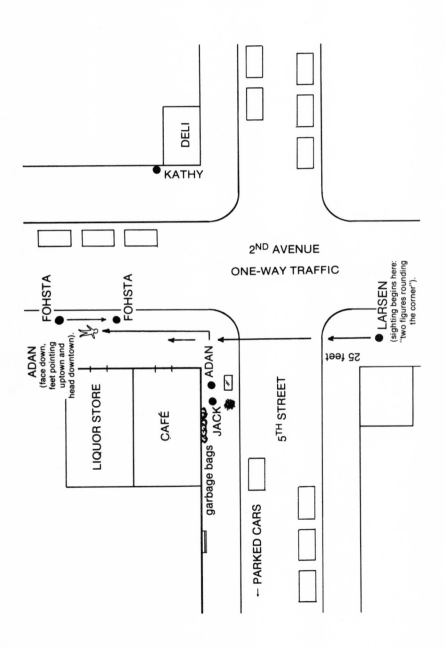

Appendix I, Section 2, A

Key:

Waiter = W
Susan = S
Veronique = V
Adan = A
Jack = J
Customers = C
Pedestrian = P

Note to Appendix

The table Abbott and his friends were seated at had a square table top. It was small, about 2' x 2'. Adan was standing opposite Veronique and facing her at all times. He was at an equal distance from Abbott and Susan. He could have as easily placed his other hand on Susan's shoulder at the same time he had his hand on Abbott's shoulder. All the time Adan was at the table he did not lean down when he spoke to Abbott or to Susan. He stood erect and did not shift his body or move from where he was standing.

(1) A lays menus on table and stands still.

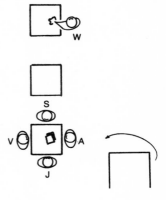

(2) S and V pick up menus. J does not pick up a menu. J has the temerity to ask for bacon, eggs, and black coffee. A replies, "I don't take orders." A places his left hand on J's shoulder, to silence J as J tries to speak. V, S, and J all look at each other bewilderedly.

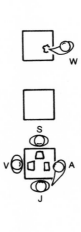

(3) S and V look at J quizzically. All three look at A quizzically. Why is he just standing there then? J asks him, "If you don't take orders, who does? Why are you standing there?"

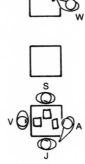

(4) A points to W and says, "See that guy over there?" J is trying to pull his shoulder away from A's hand.

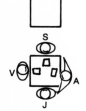

(5) J, S, and V all crane around to look where A is pointing. W looks at them. A lectures, "That's the guy that takes the orders." J squirms to get A's hand off him.

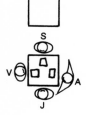

(6) W approaches and stands behind S. A releases J and steps back.

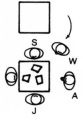

(7) S and V are discussing the menu. W takes J's order. W waits for S and V to decide what to order. A takes a position by the end of the counter.

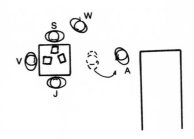

(8) C looks between A and J apprehensively. J glances over at A. A then says, "What are you looking at?"

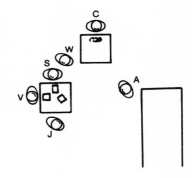

(9) A repeatedly asks, "What are you looking at?" and when J finally answers, "What? What?" A starts to walk back to their (J, V, S) table.

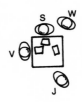

(10) J rises and walks toward A, and A steps back and waits for J at end of counter.

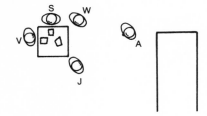

(11) A and J arguing; W approaching. A says, "Do you want to leave? Do you want me to put you out of here?"

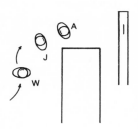

(12) W passing around them. J replies, "You don't have to tell me what to do."

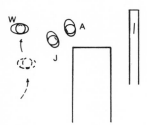

(13) J stops W, never turning away
from or taking his eyes off A.

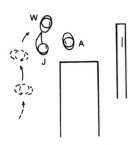

(14) As J stops W, A turns away
quickly, stepping toward shelf. It is
only three steps away.

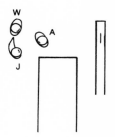

(15) J asks W, "What is wrong with
him?" W is distracted.

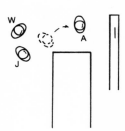

(16) W replies, "Don't pay attention to him." J keeps watching A.

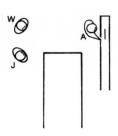

(17) A returns. A only stepped
away for a second. W starts moving
on.

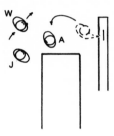

(18) As A draws closer, W backs
away somewhere. A walks up to J,
both hands in his pockets, and hits
J in the chest with his chest. J says,
"You don't have to hit me."

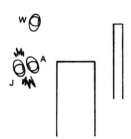

(19) A points to front door. J says, "All right, let's go outside." (etc.)

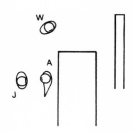

(20) Walking toward front door.

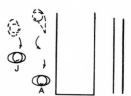

(21) At front door.

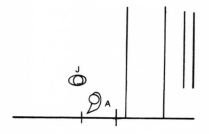

(22) A opens door with left hand, right hand still in pocket under apron (or short change-pouch).

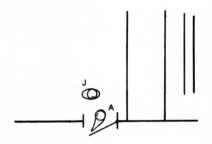

(23) C approaches as J pauses in doorway to speak to A.

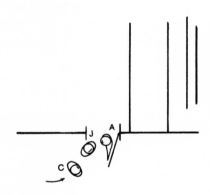

(24) J and A are blocking door as C stops.

(25) A angrily says to J, "Get going, keep moving." J moves down
sidewalk, confused. C enters.

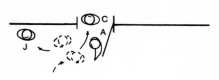

(26) J turns back to speak to A.
A releases door and says, "Keep
going." He steps toward J, shooing
him on with left hand.

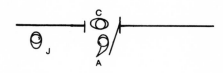

(27) J turns, confused, and takes a
step or two more.

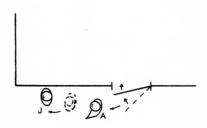

(28) J stops at corner and turns around once more. A walks toward J, shooing him with left hand.

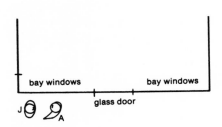

(29) Confused, J steps around corner. It is only four or five steps from door to corner. A walks to corner.

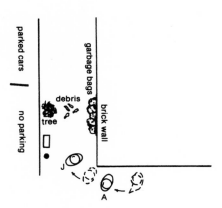

(30) J is frightened now and turns around resolved not to go further. A stands in front of side window, shooing J.

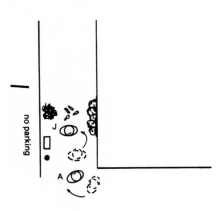

(31) J withdraws knife and shouts, "Don't come any closer! I can hear you from there." (etc.)

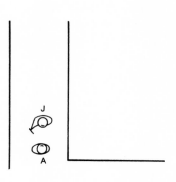

(32) A suddenly withdraws knife and springs at J as J steps toward him.

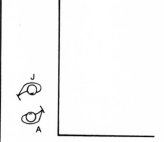

(33) J clutches A's right forearm and simultaneously stabs A. J and A collide.

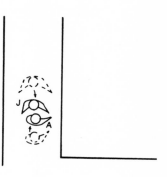

(34) A's arm goes limp and falls out of J's grip. A's knife is lost among the debris on the sidewalk.

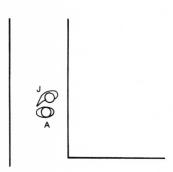

(35) J draws back knife, and A brings hands to his chest. J shouts, "Do you want some more?"

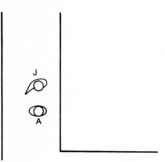

(36) A starts walking backward, in upright posture, holding chest.

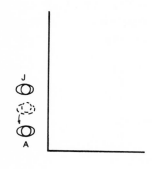

(37) J follows A as he walks backward.

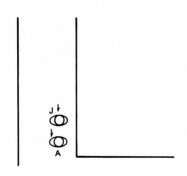

(38) J continues to follow A.

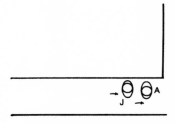

(39) J shifts knife to left hand and
reaches for A with right hand. P
approaches.

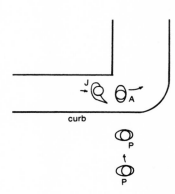

(40) A steps clear of J's hand, and
J steps back to hide as P passes.

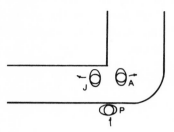

(41) J puts knife under waistband
and stands against wall as P passes.

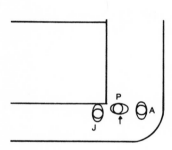

(42) J shouts for pedestrians to
stop A from walking into heavy
Second Avenue traffic.

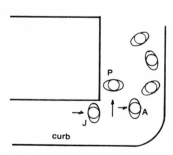

(43) At the last moment, about three feet from the curb, A turns and walks backward up Second Avenue.

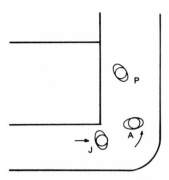

(44) J follows A.

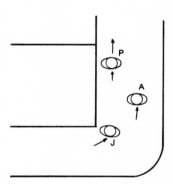

(45) A falls on face; J approaches. A crowd (five or six people) gathers immediately.

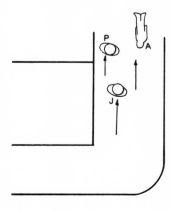

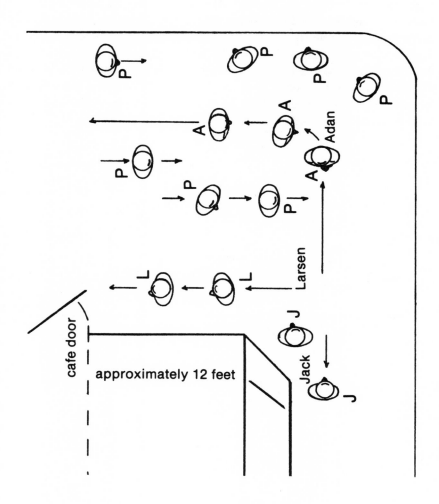

Appendix I, Section 2, C

Lighting: The lighting on Second Avenue is as bright as daylight. But there is no lighting on Fifth Street. There are a number of overflowing garbage bags against the wall. The garbage collectors pick it up every Sunday, between 5:30 and 6:00 A.M. It was picked up by the garbage collector before the police arrived. Empty bottles and cans are strewn on the sidewalk. It is very dark, especially entering Fifth Street from Second Avenue. There is one bare light bulb over the stoop of the door to a tenement apartment farther down:

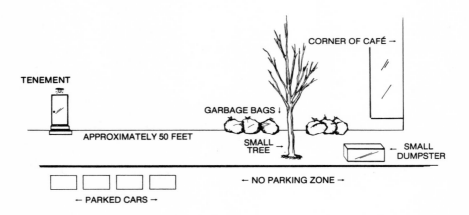

APPENDIX II
Some Information Collateral to Trial Transcript

1. Lt. Majesky's Story

Abbott waived extradition proceedings when he was arrested in Louisiana, and so he was immediately transported to New York, where he was held in the federal jail in New York City.

When the U.S. Marshals drove Abbott from the airport to the jail, they stopped at the Federal Court Building to fingerprint Abbott in Manhattan.

While a half dozen U.S. Marshals were escorting Abbott through the halls, at one point they all paused while a door was being opened. At that point the lighting in the hall was dim. Abbott was wearing handcuffs. A man reached through the crowd of U.S. Marshals and clutched Abbott's hand. Abbott glanced up to see who it was, and he heard a voice say, "Hello, Mr. Abbott." The voice was low and full of respect. The door opened, and the U.S. Marshals took him through the hall. The U.S. Marshals made vague and contemptuous remarks about the man who had tried to hold hands with Abbott. Abbott later learned that the man was William Majesky, an ex-vice-squad policeman promoted to the Homicide Division of the New York Police Department and assigned to the Ninth Precinct (in the Bowery).

About three weeks later, Abbott was handed over to the State authority of New York and released from Federal custody.

Three New York City policemen took him to the offices of the state court for fingerprinting before he was arraigned on the indictment.

While Abbott was having his fingerprints and police photographs taken, William Majesky (one of three policemen) "talked" with Abbott— along with the other policemen. This "talk" was about subjects such as the weather in New York. It lasted less than fifteen minutes. It was only small talk and had nothing to do with Abbott. After this, Abbott was taken to the elevator to be returned to the prisoner holding cell, where his lawyer was waiting. While they were waiting for a few seconds for the elevator to arrive, William Majesky asked Abbott what hotel he had been staying at in New Orleans before he had moved across the river (to the West Bank). Abbott, at that point, laughed and replied, "I'll tell you if you tell me who the New York informant was."

Majesky then named one of Abbott's friends, and so Abbott told Majesky he had stayed at a cheap hotel on St. Charles Street. The elevator arrived, and no more words were ever exchanged between Abbott and Majesky. The only time Abbott ever laid eyes on him again was in the courtroom at his trial (and he was one of the five policemen who delivered Abbott over to federal custody after his trial). *Majesky at no time read Abbott his rights or tried to interrogate him.*

Yet this Lt. William Majesky told journalists and others that he interrogated (or "interviewed") Abbott many (or "several") times. Peter Manso, the writer, reports that Majesky makes these claims.*

It is our information that this policeman solicited film producers to buy options on the film rights to his life story as a "crime fighter" and eventually succeeded in selling the option for an advance of five thousand dollars.† The information Majesky purported to have about Abbott as privileged information was protected from everyone else by the Privacy Act. The money, of course, did not go to the Crime Victim's Board—as does any money made by people who write about or sell the story of their own crimes—but into Majesky's pocket. The ironies are endless.

Majesky, as investigating officer, had the right to demand to be allowed to search through police and institution files on Abbott. These materials are not available under ordinary circumstances, in keeping with the Privacy Act. Using his authority Majesky was able to gather this information. Abbott, however, has a standing offer and has made it to several media outlets: Abbott will cooperate with any media representative to gather all files and information in existence about him, under the Freedom of Information Act. Abbott has already made this offer to the ABC national television network. Abbott is forced to make this offer only because of the circulation of false and slanderous information, which no one can verify except through sources like Majesky.

Majesky told Alan King (another film producer) that he did not want anyone to make a hero out of Abbott. Majesky no doubt sold the rights to his life story thinking the producers were going to make a hero out of him.

The New Orleans Police Department reports that sightings of Abbott in the city were quite frequent, sometimes two or three a day. Abbott had no idea he had become a highly publicized media event, for the simple reason that his first month as a fugitive was in the backwaters of Mexico. So he did not try to disguise his appearance. There was no "New York informant."

Lt. Majesky used a telephone in New York to "investigate" Abbott outside of New York City. There were at least a dozen witnesses at the "scene of the crime," and Lt. Majesky only picked out Larsen, who was probably the only white ex-Marine there. He neglected to record the names of the others.

---

* *Mailer: His Life and Times,* Simon and Schuster, New York, 1985, pp. 636-7.
† *Los Angeles Times,* December 26, 1982. Ellen Farley conducted the interview with Majesky and the producers, Eric Bercovici and Lee Savin (MGM-United Artists).

2. Larsen's Story

View down Fifth Street of the Cooper Square Restaurant (remodeled from the Binibon). The doorway to the Binibon was closer to the corner of the block than is the door of the Cooper Square Restaurant. The Binibon's doorway was situated in the center of the café and was no more than ten feet from the corner.

One of the components of Larsen's story is that his sister was engaged to marry a Puerto Rican ex-convict, whom Larsen found irritating and could not get along with. That was the crux of his argument with them earlier that evening when he left them and began wandering the streets (for about ten hours) until he walked into the incident with Abbott. Larsen (blond, blue-eyed) had serious reservations about his sister marrying the ex-convict.

But when Larsen returned from Texas, about a week before he testified, Abbott sent someone to his sister's apartment. She had seen Larsen. He had been to her place and had a copy of Abbott's book (*In the Belly of the Beast*) and was citing passages to her to explain to her why he could not get along with her fiancé. He left the book with her. The book was worn from use.

Abbott attacked proud Vietnam veterans in the book, which may have antagonized Larsen: He was a proud Vietnam veteran, a Marine.

Larsen spent an inordinate amount of time alone with Majesky, the detective in charge of the investigation; and, at one point, it is suggested that Majesky may have been instrumental in finding him employment, since he had found a job for witness Fohsta. The evening before he testified, Larsen and Majesky drove around talking for two hours in Majesky's car.

In numerous telephone interviews, Lt. Majesky told Ruby, a woman Abbott was with in New Orleans, that Abbott was a psychopath who had killed about six men and that Abbott was a heroin addict and a homosexual. He told her that Adan was one of "Abbott's homosexual contacts." He told her that he had been studying Abbott's entire life. Majesky also told this to George Griffin, someone Abbott had met in Mexico. Griffin was in Alaska when Majesky telephoned him. For what it is worth, there is nothing in any police or prison files on Abbott that even suggests homosexuality, or any sexual subject. The only purpose this sexual slander served was to horrify anyone who wanted to bring reasonable understanding to the affair. It served to alienate Jack's friends and totally isolate him.

Neither Ruby nor George knew about Abbott's life. They were only with him several days Ruby was with Abbott seven days; George was with Abbott six days: George and Ruby did not know each other and to this day have never seen or spoken to each other. Yet they have both, in taped interviews, related exactly the same account of Majesky's behavior and words. There is evidence that Majesky also told people in New York this same misinformation. So it is probable he told this to Larsen as well. Except for their own personal experiences with Abbott, no one had any way of knowing that Majesky was falsifying. If he never told Larsen these things, then Larsen was the only one he never told these things to.

Majesky is presently silent on all this, possibly because of fear of legal action on account of his utterances. George and Ruby said that Majesky threatened to charge them with aiding and abetting a fugitive if they communicated with Abbott.

3. Burdes's Story

Burdes was a waiter in the Deli Stop across the street. He did not know Adan but called him "Richie." The waiter in the Binibon did not know Adan either; he knew Adan only as his boss.

First of all, Burdes testified that Adan talked to him for ten minutes before the ambulance arrived.* Pain and suffering in a "wrongful death"

---

*Burdes could not recall even one word he or Adan spoke during the alleged conversation. He could not recall the nature or even the subject of the conversa-

lawsuit are calculated by time. Adan was dead on arrival at the hospital. Doctors examined him and reported that he died in seconds. His heart was severed in two.

Second, Burdes testified that there were no menus at the Binibon. It is true there were no menus at the deli where he worked, but the Binibon did use menus. Third, he testified that the Binibon had no air conditioner when in fact it did. Finally, he testified that Binibon customers were sent to urinate around the corner on Fifth Street. The photograph of the (remodeled) Binibon (attached to Larsen's story) was taken from the entrance to the deli where Burdes was employed. Burdes testified that Binibon customers were allowed to use the restroom in the deli but that some of them were told they could pee on the sidewalk on Fifth Street. This was (typically) another untruth.

The police in charge of the investigation looked into Burdes's story and rejected it. The prosecutor at the trial stipulated to the court that he rejected Burdes's story, and it slipped out in Burdes's "testimony."

In addition to this, we are asked to believe that the night manager left one waiter in charge of a café filled with customers while he took a customer around the corner on Fifth Street to show him where to urinate on the sidewalk. The Binibon waiter had no idea why Adan went outside. In his opinion, Adan kicked Abbott out.

Burdes had to have lied when he testified to the impossible: that Adan talked to him for ten minutes after he had been stabbed. Being charitable, we can assume he was merely mistaken when he asserted that the Binibon had no individual menus and that there was no air conditioner. And so we can assume he was merely mistaken and not deliberately lying about the non-existent policy of the Binibon sending customers to pee outside on the sidewalk, however ill-lit Fifth Street was.

Burdes said that the Binibon had no air conditioner when in fact it did have an air conditioner that made a loud noise when it came on. The air conditioner unit was sticking out by the corner of the café on Fifth Street. It is present in the photograph opposite.

---

tion. Nor did he describe an evocation of emotions. Fohsta (and others) hovered over Adan until the ambulance arrived and did not report that Adan uttered a sound (or moved).

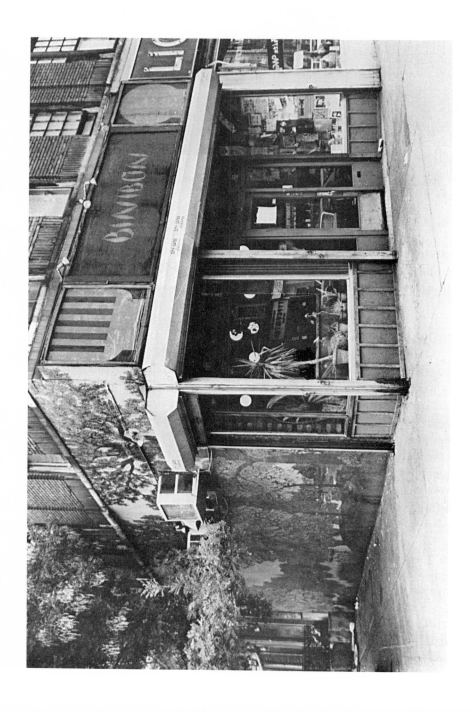

This is a photograph of the Deli Stop where Burdes worked. The photo was taken on the corner where Larsen was standing when he started across Fifth Street (on Second Avenue). The arched doorway beside the Deli Stop arches over the stoop that Kathy, the witness, was sitting on when she observed the scene.

4. Swartzchild's (The Waiter's) Story

Roger Swartzchild was the waiter at the Binibon. When Swartzchild approached to be sworn in before testifying at the trial, he grew suspicious and demanded to know if the Bible was a Christian Bible. He refused to take the oath until the bailiff assured him it was indeed a Christian Bible. He was twenty years of age. When the police arrived and interviewed him, he told them that Adan appeared to be blocking the way for Abbott to go into the kitchen. Somewhere in the kitchen basement was an employees' restroom. He *inferred* that the argument was over access to the restroom. He was very busy while the incident between Adan and Abbott was taking place, but when he testified before the grand jury, before Abbott was captured, he went to great lengths to elaborate his assumption that the dispute was over access to the restroom. Later, at the trial, his testimony was totally different. He retracted all he had said to the grand jury and admitted that he had merely assumed all he had testified to at the grand jury.

But at the grand jury he was asked if he knew any reason why Adan would have gone outside with Abbott. He could not imagine why, except that Adan was putting Abbott out of the café for misbehaving. He was definite at the grand jury that it was not Adan but Abbott who made the challenge to step outside. He was just as definite about this at Abbott's trial. And at the time he testified at the grand jury, he was basing all his testimony on assumptions. Had there been a policy to send customers outside to urinate, it would have entered his assuming mind that Adan had directed Abbott to go outside to urinate. Yet he was baffled and could only assume that Adan had told Abbott to leave and that Abbott had refused to leave and had challenged Adan to "step outside."

Swartzchild had worked in the café for one month prior to this. He testified that he had never seen Adan fight with anyone, although he had seen Adan regularly force customers to leave the café. The fact is, a week prior to the incident with Abbott, four men got into an argument inside the café. Swartzchild may not have been present. Adan ordered them to leave and threatened them with violence if they did not leave. They left. But as soon as they were outside, they began fighting with each other on the sidewalk in front of the café. Adan called the police, then stepped out onto the sidewalk and intervened forcibly to stop the fight. The police arrived. This incident is in the Ninth Precinct records, and the employees of the Deli Stop across the street observed this fracas. A man named "Marty" (who worked at the Deli Stop with Burdes) told investigators that fights routinely took place at the café across the street.

Burdes was about twenty years of age and a native of that neighborhood of Manhattan. Marty was almost sixty years of age.

These photographs were taken at the scene of the stabbing on Fifth Street where the remodeled Binibon now sits, now under new ownership and called Cooper Square Restaurant. The canopied windows in these photographs were not present in the Binibon at the time of the stabbing. The photographs were taken on a Sunday morning, between 5:30 and 6:00 A.M., just before the city garbage collector removed the garbage bags. As is evident, there are a number of full garbage bags. The stabbing occurred at some point on the sidewalk between the tree and the fire hydrant.

APPENDIX III
Notes on the Play

1. The quotations quoted were public. José Torres, Erroll McDonald, and Norris Church Mailer all made their remarks to Peter Manso, as material for his book, *Mailer: His Life and Times.* Mailer's "seed of evil" remark was made on national television and repeated on *60 Minutes,* during the Ed Bradley interview.

2. The quotations of Lt. William Majesky also came from a taped interview by Peter Manso, recorded in his book on Norman Mailer.

3. *Note on the killer vignette:* As a vignette, Abbott wrote a description of a man being murdered in a prison cell. Abbott's description was *designed* to charge the emotions of the reader. He graphically describes the thoughts and feelings of both the victim and the killer. He also describes graphically the *physical movements* of the victim and the killer. In the blur of emotions, the reader tends to ignore the physical action described. Therefore this note is meant to illuminate the physical movements.

The two men (alone in a prison cell) are facing each other in a standing position. The killer looks at the victim's chest and sees the "target": "You see the spot. It's a target between the second and third button on his shirt."

Before the killer looks at the "target," he slips out a knife and holds it beside his leg so that the victim does not notice it.

After looking at the "target," the killer moves his "left foot to the side." In doing this, he "steps across" the *victim's* "right-side body length."

None of these physical movements is at all strange. They are exactly the same physical moves a man makes to slug another man in the face with a right-cross punch, except his fist holds a knife and he is "punching" him in the chest.

In sequence, then, here are the graphics of the movements and positions:

"... his right-side body length"   "... slipped out a knife ... holding it beside your leg ..."

VICTIM   KILLER

The killer is facing the victim:

The killer moves his "left foot to the side, to step across his right-side body length."

(1)   (2)   (3)

left foot →

"A light pivot toward him with your right shoulder ... you have sunk the knife in ..."

In the action of the play, synchronize the killer vignette with the Prosecutor and notes on a cello:

When, in Act III, the Prosecutor finishes his line: ". . . IT IS LIKE CUTTING HOT BUTTER, NO RESISTENCE AT ALL.—Did you write that, Mr. Abbott? Did you? Did you?" and before Abbott answers, LEADER picks it up and completes the vignette:

LEADER
With deep feeling.
THEY ALWAYS WHISPER ONE THING AT THE END: PLEASE. YOU GET THE ODD IMPRESSION HE IS NOT IMPLORING YOU NOT TO HARM HIM, BUT TO DO IT RIGHT. IF HE SAYS YOUR NAME, IT SOFTENS YOUR RESOLVE. YOU GO INTO A STUPOR OF SORTS. THINGS REGISTER IN SLOW MOTION, BECAUSE ALL YOUR SENSES ARE DRAWN TO A NEW HEIGHT. YOU LEAVE HIM IN THE BLOOD, STARING WITH DEAD EYES. BUT YOU WANT TO STOP IN THE MIDDLE OF IT . . .
Here the actor drops the knife and enacts the following.
. . . AND HOLD HIM SO TIGHT YOU CAN FORCE HIS LIFE BACK INTO HIM AND SAVE HIM. BUT YOU CAN'T TURN AROUND IN THE MIDDLE OF IT. IT'S THE UNREASON OF VIOLENCE, THIS TIME IN FAVOR OF LIFE, THAT TRIES TO STOP YOU IN THE ACT—THE SAME FORCE THAT BROUGHT YOU TO THIS ACT.

The killer stabs the victim five or six times before the victim falls to the floor. Once on the floor, the killer falls to his knees and stabs him methodically on the floor. Then he drops the knife and tries to lift the body into a sitting position. It should be as graphic as possible. The actors vanish in darkness; cello stops; ABBOTT answers the question PROSECUTOR puts to him.

ABBOTT
It's good, isn't it . . . (etc.)

APPENDIX IV
A Note on the Trial

Abbott's Defense

When Abbott was arrested, he explained to those who knew him in New York, through notes and telephone conversations, what had happened, and he told them all (including his lawyer) that he'd stabbed Adan with a knife he'd been carrying.

In his opening address to the jury his lawyer asserted that Adan was stabbed with Adan's own knife. He stated to the jury that Adan had picked up a knife, put it in his pocket, and that he was stabbed with it. In his closing address he apologized for telling the jury something he knew was not true.

Before the trial, Abbott had decided not to testify. It was on that condition that the prosecutor agreed not to use his book, *In the Belly of the Beast,* against him. But when his lawyer told these things to the jury, he began to privately reconsider his decision not to testify.

When Abbott heard his lawyer ask the jury, in his closing address, to find Abbott guilty of First Degree Manslaughter, Abbott began to contemplate dismissing him and finding another lawyer for the appeal. Then when Abbott did not hear his lawyer ask the jury to acquit him, it deepened his resolve to do so. Abbott testified to having acted in self-defense. While it is true that Abbott is not a lawyer and might not have understood his lawyer correctly, this is in fact what convinced Abbott to resolutely dismiss his lawyer for his appeal. He did dismiss his lawyer several times outside the courtroom for not thoroughly cross-examining witnesses. He had to re-hire him each time, however, because he feared the press would publish a misinterpretation of the circumstances if Abbott represented himself mid-trial.

Abbott insisted on testifying. Other than his testimony, no evidence was presented in his defense.

The Prosecutor's Intention

In his opening address to the jury, the prosecutor merely read the indictment and did not state what facts he intended to prove. Abbott had no idea what he would contend, except, perhaps, that the argument with Adan was over access to a restroom, since the newspapers were screaming this out all over the country. It is not inconceivable that an argument could occur over such a thing, and the mere fact that it was an argument was all that seemed relevant to Abbott. Even so, he was not willing to accept that Adan thought he wanted to use the restroom. The prosecutor made *no* contention whatsoever as to facts in his opening address. None at all.

Manslaughter in this setting (two men arguing) merely means, in law, that two men argue and fight, and in the heat of the altercation one of them formulates an intent to kill; he goes *beyond* subduing his opponent and kills him deliberately and in anger. This is what First Degree Manslaughter is in the State of New York. In common usage, it is plain *manslaughter.*

Involuntary manslaughter in this setting means, in law, that two men argue and fight, and one *accidentally* kills the other. In the State of New York this is termed Second Degree Manslaughter. In common usage throughout America it is plain *involuntary manslaughter* and is almost a misdemeanor offense.

This is true of both degrees of manslaughter, regardless of whether or not a *weapon* (or weapons) is involved. Very seldom are weapons *not* involved in manslaughter, and usually the weapon (or weapons) is a knife, gun, or bludgeoning instrument. The mere *fact* that someone has died is no *proof* of an intent to kill. That is not what the indictment implies. One cannot prove something about an event by presupposing about the event what remains to be proven.

The police made no search of the area for weapons. But it does not matter whether or not Adan had a weapon, although the evidence suggests that he did. If anyone is threatened in the streets with violence or force, he has the right to use enough force to ward off an attack, regardless of whether his attacker is armed or unarmed. And he has the right to use a knife or a gun, or *any* weapon, to turn away *any* attack (armed or unarmed).

Abbott did not engage in a fist fight with Adan, and Abbott warned Adan to stay back when Adan lunged at him, brandishing a knife (which it is suggested may have been a "butter knife") to frighten him away from the café. Adan had no right to follow Abbott outside and order him, with threats of force, to walk down the sidewalk.

The police at Riker's Island Jail, after the trial, explained that it is common in Manhattan for café managers to do this (especially in the

Bowery), and it was explained that it was common for café managers to pick up a weapon to intimidate someone who is reluctant to leave when ordered to do so. Abbott had only heard of such behavior in "knock-down drag-out" beer halls. He had no conception whatsoever of such behavior in cafés, particularly since this café did not serve any form of alcoholic beverages. He was told it was common only after his trial.

The problem developed at the table in the café because Adan, after laying down the menus, simply stood there over them. When he refused to take Abbott's "orders" (and remained standing there) it caused them all confusion and raised the question of *why* he was standing over them. When he put his hand on Abbott, Abbott reacted. It jolted him. He *was* irritated by all this. Then, when Abbott was trying to reason with Adan and stopped the waiter in the midst of it, Adan thought Abbott was now "harassing" his waiter, which, from his point of view, Abbott was. The café was busy, and this was the only waiter. Abbott was attempting to get the waiter to intervene in some way.

Adan's Myth

Susan Roxas and Roger Swartzchild testified at Abbott's trial as to the nature of the exchanges that took place between Adan and Abbott before they went outside. They were the only witnesses of this.

Swartzchild (the waiter) testified that Adan was speaking to Abbott in a harsh tone of voice, even though Swartzchild did not pick up all that was being said because he was busy passing back and forth serving customers. He heard some of it, however, and what he heard was violent, angry. Indeed, when Swartzchild originally drew the false inference that Abbott was trying to get to the restroom, it was because of the forceful manner in which Adan was confronting Abbott. Swartzchild at the time *assumed* that Adan was forcefully blocking Abbott from going to the restroom. He later testified instead that Adan appeared to be "blocking Abbott" in a confrontation. He testified to hearing Abbott say, "You don't have to push me." He testified that they were *arguing,* heatedly. Susan Roxas testified that Adan and Abbott appeared to be arguing angrily. This is the trial evidence, not interpretation.

There was absolutely no evidence presented at Abbott's trial that Adan was *not* angry and confronting Abbott forcefully. To portray Adan as having been mild and non-hostile, as having been pliant and trying to be of service, is a piece of libel that has no basis in anything except the malicious intentions of Abbott's detractors.

Adan's body was cremated within days after his death. The ashes were taken to rest in the Philippine islands. His wife was a native of the Philippines. The autopsy photographs of Adan's body were misplaced in the coroner's offices and were never found.

A routine autopsy was performed on Adan within hours of his death. Later that day the initial police investigation revealed that Adan was known to abuse a barbiturate drug. That afternoon a second autopsy was performed, with the specific purpose of determining if he had abused the drug recently. The tests proved negative. However, it was positively determined that Adan had been smoking marijuana before his death. Abbott was told there was no need for this information, because marijuana does not have the effect of transforming the user into a psychopathic maniac.

The press has tried to construct a picture of Adan's character that would exonerate him from *any* facts. Adan was living in semi-poverty in a two-room apartment on the Lower East Side, which he shared with his wife and three other adults. Adan had been married for less than six months and they had no children. He was born in Cuba, raised in Miami, and lived a while in New Jersey before going to Manhattan. His wife was studying acting in the "small theaters" on the Lower East Side (usually rented store-fronts and empty tenement buildings). Adan got involved in the craft of acting, which included attempts at writing plays. One must understand scripts. He was neither a playwright nor a choreographer. In Manhattan (two square miles of land) there are over one hundred thousand actors belonging to unions and about two hundred thousand actors who do not belong to unions.

Adan had only a minor's education and had always been a full-time employee at the café. It was not a part-time job. The press tried to portray the café as an artists' hangout, and again this was not true. It was a neighborhood eatery for poor people and derelicts.

So far we have merely pointed out a few of the misrepresentations of Adan that were unleashed on the public in order to discredit Abbott. We have cited facts and a few statistics. Whether or not Adan's character included what critics call "tragic flaws" is a question best left for the critics to decide. We have not remarked on Adan's character. But a remark should be made. It is known by those concerned enough to inquire. Those who knew Adan report that he was aggressive and impatient with strangers. Timidity was not a character trait anyone attributed to Adan, nor has anyone described him as having a sunny disposition.

But the press, using homosexual baiting, has used Adan's association with the theater as a device to project him as a passive, effete, "too pretty" young boy who could not possibly have done what witnesses testify that he did. (Small theater in the Lower East Side is hardly a "gay profession" at any rate.) While it is beside the point, Adan was not a homosexual, nor did he associate with homosexuals. Adan was rehearsing for a role in a benefit play at the time. The play closed after three performances. His role was of a stereotyped Puerto Rican street-gang member. While Adan played different characters, his specialty was in fact the macho "tough guy" role. Abbott was told this before his trial, and he was told that Adan may have been "acting" at the time—testing his role. At that point Abbott was susceptible to this nonsense, so when he testified that he took Adan for a hoodlum (and elaborated the stereotype), Abbott failed to connect it in his mind to what he had previously testified to in praise of Adan's acting. Abbott did not have a chance to correct the misunderstanding.

Our information on Adan since Abbott's conviction (obtained by investigators and interviews with Adan's New York relatives) does not at all preclude Abbott's perceptions of Adan's behavior that night, however.

But, in any case, Adan was twenty-two years old, a grown man. Statistics verify that most crimes of violence in the streets are committed by men in his age group (eighteen to twenty-four). He had lived in a violent section of the city for about two years. He knew the streets. He was the same age as the "Son of Sam" killer. He outweighed Abbott by almost fifty pounds.

It was Abbott who knew nothing about Bowery behavior.

Here in the United States of America, police report twenty-three thousand homicides every year. Most of these homicides are accidental deaths arising out of conflicts identical to the kind that erupted between Adan and Abbott, and no one is punished for them.

Abbott's Life Sentence

In America no prior conviction that is over ten years old can be used against a defendant in a court of law.

Every state has "habitual criminal" statutes. A person who is repeatedly convicted for serious crimes and is in and out of prison for new convictions for years *may* be placed under the *status* of habitual criminal by the prosecutor. But it has to be justified by proving a pattern of *convictions,* and very seldom is a man placed under this status. There is a code of law under this status. The laws in this special-status code are violated merely upon the return of a verdict of guilty. The convicted man is sentenced for the crime he was convicted of, and then a new set of proceedings ensues, because now he has also violated a law under the special status. The prosecutor establishes the status, and the court sentences the man again by aggravating his sentence for conviction of the crime.

He is given a life sentence, even though the crime he was convicted of carries only a few years' imprisonment.

This is considered a highly unusual occurrence. It has been done to only a few men. In fact, most men in prison today between the ages of thirty and forty have up to four and five convictions and have been in prison four or five times (for new convictions). This even includes serious convictions involving rape, homicide, and assault within ten years.

Yet, it was done to Abbott. He was given a life sentence.

Abbott was originally sent to prison for a crime that is today a misdemeanor—issuing a check against insufficient funds. He deliberately overdrew his own bank account.

In prison, he was convicted of "Assault by Convict Without Malice Aforethought." This law, under which he was convicted, was repealed by the Utah State Legislature in 1973 because it was too general and included mere possession of a weapon in prison. Abbott was *factually* convicted of possession of a weapon in prison. He was acquitted, on the basis of self-defense, of the charge of the murder of one of the two men involved in a prison "altercation" with him when he was twenty-one (on January 10, 1966).

The "Assault by Convict Without Malice Aforethought" conviction was used in 1982 in New York to put Abbott under the special status of a habitual criminal—sixteen years later.

When Abbott escaped from prison for six weeks, in March 1971, he held up a bank teller in Denver and was tried and sent to Leavenworth. The gun was empty, no shot was fired, and no one was hurt. But this conviction was also used to put him under the special status—eleven years later.

A complicated and involved method of calculation of years was put forward by the prosecutor to offer a semblance of *legal* validity to it all. But it remains illegal. Abbott was given a sentence of life imprisonment for conviction of a crime that carries no more than six years' imprisonment on the justification that he was a habitual criminal who had been in and out of prison for serious crimes too often. However, his parole to New York was the first time he had ever been released or paroled from prison since he first went to prison for a minor offense at age eighteen. He had no convictions other than the two described above.

The Prosecutor's Contentions

The prosecutor at no time offered Abbott a plea negotiation before the trial. It was never clear what facts in particular the prosecutor was trying to prove or assert. When Abbott took the witness stand, the prosecutor did not question him about the charge he was on trial for.

All through the melange of testimony that the prosecutor was offering as evidence, it was never clear what *facts* he was trying to bring out. There was no testimony about a restroom. I doubt that, even today, he or the judge would be able to state a clear contention of facts about this matter. On the one hand, the waiter did not testify that it was a dispute over the restroom but suggested that Abbott was being asked to leave for unruly behavior. On the other hand, the prosecutor presented a floor-plan of the café and asked the waiter to point out where Abbott and his friends were seated. Without being asked by the Prosecutor, the waiter (without explanation) pointed out that the café had a restroom which was entered by going through the kitchen and down a flight of stairs. It was the only time the waiter ever mentioned a restroom. This testimony was given as an after-thought without verbal prompting from the prosecutor. When Larsen testified, he rattled off his testimony as if he were reciting *The Raven*. When Abbott took the witness stand, the prosecutor simply questioned him about his nineteen-year prison record and then read passages out of context from a book he wrote.

It should be noted that interviews with the jurors after the verdict confirm that the jury believed the facts were not nearly as exotic as Abbott's friends report. The jury decided that Adan and Abbott argued and stepped outside to settle it, that Adan took a swing at Abbott with his fist, and that Abbott responded with a knife-thrust that killed him. In itself this is not against the law since Abbott did not intend to kill Adan. It is not against the law to pull out a knife in self-defense against someone who is attacking, even if he is attacking without a weapon. The jury was convinced that Abbott was a "dangerous man," but the jury did not entertain the idea that he was emotionally disturbed. Of course, any jury finding (of facts) of diminished capacity (including "emotional disturbance") does not merely lessen the degree of criminal culpability: It *acquits* the accused of any crime. It is the *judge* who may consider emotional disturbance as an extenuating factor in the punishment (as a matter of *law*). This was not done in Abbott's case. The jury rejected Larsen's testimony and accepted Abbott's account.

The jury also believed that Abbott had expertise with a knife and previous convictions for murdering people. Both were false assumptions. The jury believed Abbott was predisposed to kill merely from the book he'd written and from hearsay information about his life taken from news items (not police or prison records).

At the time, Abbott could not believe it was possible that he could be tried in the manner he was tried, in front of more than seventy news journalists. In trying to make sense of the medley of innuendo the prosecutor was offering, and under pressure from a total lack of information, he collapsed when a waiter from the deli across the street from the café testified that the café sometimes sent customers to urinate on Fifth Street (which was not true).

Up to that point, Abbott had been unable to comprehend why the press made much ado over the idea that it was an argument precisely over the use of a restroom. Abbott thought that it could not have been pertinent what the argument was about, because he did not know Adan.

Abbott's lawyer convinced Abbott that Abbott had misinterpreted Adan's words and behavior. Abbott's lawyer did not advise Abbott that it was a reasonable possibility that Adan was kicking Abbott out of the café. Abbott had no concept of being thrown out of the café. He thought Adan was taking him outside to talk about his problem. Abbott thought it could be settled without a fight.

So the deli waiter's testimony shattered Abbott. He could not stop shaking, and his nerves collapsed. *At that time,* he insisted on testifying, in a shattered condition. He was incompetent when he took the stand.

The prosecutor, in his closing remarks to the jury, offered up his melange once more, but this time he added to it bits and pieces from Abbott's testimony.

The most damaging construction possible is the following:

Wayne Larsen's Uncorroborated Testimony

Larsen was inconsistent throughout the trial, despite what Abbott's friends say. His testimony was subjective, emotional impressions that have no place in a trial transcript.

After stating that he saw Adan and Abbott round the corner and saw

Adan go suddenly into reverse (walking backward), Larsen then went on to draw *illegal* inferences, which were not objected to. Larsen was almost one hundred feet away, across the street, when the incident occurred. In court, Larsen was asked to further describe this "walking backward," and he said that Adan's hands were in front of him, "as if to say, 'I've had enough.' " Larsen went on in this "as if to say" manner a great deal. The implication was that Adan was trying to disengage from a fight. Larsen said he could hear *nothing*.

Larsen testified that, at the corner, Adan stopped walking backward and turned and walked back to the café door. The café door was only four or five steps away from the corner. Larsen never testified about where he was when all this was taking place.

Out on the street, the air conditioner unit over Abbott's head came on, making a sharp noise. It startled Abbott too, and he was not sure if it was the air conditioner unit or a car backfiring or a newspaper truck dropping a bundle of papers. But it was irrelevant to him.

However, Larsen said he saw a "flash." He *inferred* that it was a knife. His testimony is full of such descriptive adjectives. He even said that he had nightmares about it, it was so horrible to him, a Marine who saw active service in Vietnam. He then testified that Abbott "lunged" forward, and the "flash" of the knife disappeared around Adan, while Adan's *back* was to Abbott. Then he heard a loud "bang" which he said haunted him a long time afterward. And he inferred from these three impressions that Adan was stabbed at the time of the sharp noise or loud bang (which was irrelevant, for Abbott has never denied stabbing Adan). Larsen said that Abbott then "recoiled" and "taunted" Adan "sadistically." All three inferences were subjective impressions and not *facts*. He testified that Adan let forth a stream of fairly eloquent sentences which he proceeded to quote verbatim: "I told you I do not want any more trouble." "Please leave me alone." Et cetera.

Larsen stated that while Adan clutched at his chest and backed away somewhere, Abbott stood still and "taunted" him "sadistically," but Larsen never quoted a word Abbott supposedly said. Nor did he "infer" any quotations. He described Abbott's stance as if he were Dracula emanating menacing, powerful "magic rays." After some time of this, with Abbott *not moving a single step,* Larsen testified, Adan fell to the sidewalk, and Abbott, suddenly empty-handed, went over and looked at him and then fled.

The front of the café was entirely glass, and the waiter testified that when Adan and Abbott walked out he started watching out the bay window. He saw Adan come from around the corner, cross the front of the café, and collapse in front of the liquor store by the curb.

Fohsta testified that he was there on the sidewalk and only saw Adan walking backward (hands over chest) to collapse on the sidewalk.

Kathy testified that she was sitting on a stoop facing the café. She saw Adan emerge from Fifth Street (holding his chest) and collapse on Second Avenue.

Abbott and Adan were under observation at all times.

All three eyewitnesses contradicted Larsen's testimony and confirmed Abbott's.

The prosecutor's accusation that Abbott constructed his testimony from Larsen's is weakened by the fact that Abbott was not present in court when Larsen testified (as well as by the fact that Abbott had written several friends and related what happened). He had asked to be excused.

The worst construction having now been aired, what do we have?

We have a picture of a man in a rage (Abbott) and a second man (Adan) trying to get away from him. The prosecutor, incidentally, in his melange, attempted to assert that a small abrasion that Adan sustained on his face when he fell to the sidewalk was sustained instead by the blow of a fist. So there was a *fight* he was trying to disengage from. This would mean that the man in the rage had been fighting the second man. The second man had had enough and was trying to get away.

But the man in the rage suddenly, *at that point,* withdraws a knife for the first time and gives chase. He runs up to the second man, and, to hear Larsen tell it, with some secret *ninja*-like knowledge of the esoteric art of murder, manages, from behind the second man, to plant a knife in the exact center of his chest. Not at an angle, either, but perpendicular to the surface of his chest. Straight in and straight out. The wound was clean. A pathetic way to make a "back-stabber" out of Abbott!

But even this is beside the point.

He stabs the man one time.

Then he stands still and curses him in a loud voice while the other man holds his wound and pleads with him not to hurt him, moving away at the same time. All this in front of a café with three eyewitnesses who reported seeing *none* of it.

Under the circumstances, what Larsen testified to would have taken a long time.

But let's not belabor this either.

The man who stabbed the other man *makes no move toward him* after stabbing him once, over all this time. He stands still and "taunts" him while the second man "pleads." A dialogue. The man who is stabbed is very articulate, even eloquent.

This describes a man with a very nasty temper whom the other man wishes he had never laid eyes on.

But it does not describe an intent to kill. Even if we suppose he "intended" to kill him when he stabbed him, the fact that he stood still and had a shouting-match with him after stabbing him disproves any intent to kill.

And this is one of the reasons the jury rejected Larsen's testimony and acquitted Abbott of Murder. Other than Larsen, Abbott was the only witness to testify to the act of Adan's being wounded. Larsen did not testify to having actually seen Abbott stab Adan. He testified that he "reasonably inferred" Adan was stabbed after he saw a "flash" (which looked like a knife) and heard a loud "bang!" (which sounded like a blow).

We have the right to speculate as to why Larsen felt it was important to establish that Abbott stabbed Adan. Larsen could have had the impression that Abbott had supporters who were powerful. He could have had the impression that Abbott would beat the charge through fancy legal manipulations. He could have had the impression that if no one testified to having actually *seen* Abbott stab Adan then Abbott's fancy lawyers and powerful friends would get Abbott off the hook. We know that Larsen thought Abbott denied having stabbed Adan. He thought it had to be proved.

He could have reasonably inferred that Adan (since he was in fact stabbed) *must* have been stabbed at some point while he was observing them. The problem would have presented itself *to him* as a problem of analyzing his impressions of the memory. From this "self-examination" he made his inferences.

From our speculations, we too may "reasonably infer" what Larsen was doing. As Larsen paused at the curb before crossing Fifth Street, he glanced away from Adan and Abbott momentarily before crossing the street. It is normal to do so to be sure no cars are approaching in order to cross the street safely. In that short interim, Abbott and Adan collided and Adan was wounded. As Larsen looked back, he saw Adan "walking backward."

Then as he passed between Abbott and Adan at the corner, he was frightened as he saw Abbott tucking a knife under his waistband and stepping out onto Second Avenue, shouting for someone to stop Adan from backing into Second Avenue automobile traffic.

Larsen testified that he had visual problems and difficulties perceiving perspectives, what he referred to as "difficulties with depth perception." Larsen was not wearing his glasses that night. Approaching the café from across Fifth Street, in semi-darkness it appears that where the window ends on Fifth Street the corner begins. As one crosses the street it appears that the extension of the window on Fifth Street is instead the front of the café on Second Avenue. When Larsen saw Abbott moving past the side window on Fifth Street, he probably had the optical illusion that Abbott was moving up Second Avenue in front of the café. We have reasoned how Larsen could have been merely mistaken in what he *saw*. As for what he *heard*, he heard what all the other witnesses heard. They heard Abbott shouting at pedestrians. Adan had a one-inch hole through his heart. It is medically impossible that Adan could have delivered what amounts to eloquent speeches which Larsen claimed to quote word-for-word. Larsen testified only to impressions of Abbott shouting but he testified to hearing Adan articulate lengthy sentences after he was wounded.

In all sincerity, and with disinterested judgment, it is impossible to conclude that Larsen had merely made a *mistake* in that part of his testimony. What he was doing in his testimony was obvious to the jury, which rejected all of it. Only the press chose to pay attention to it.

The jury accepted Abbott's account because it was in accord with all other evidence and known facts. The Prosecutor argued that Abbott was guilty of Murder. He did not argue that Abbott was guilty of First Degree Manslaughter. The jury totally rejected the Prosecutor's arguments, along with Larsen's uncorroborated, subjective inferences.

Larsen's testimony as to facts could not be staged in the play because it would defy (in space and time) the facts presented by the four other prosecution witnesses and all other evidence.

No statement as to facts has been left out of the play.

Courtroom readings of select parts of *In the Belly of the Beast* (and prejudicial misinformation obtained from outside the courtroom) convinced the jury to find Abbott guilty of manslaughter. From misinformation and prejudice, the jury was convinced that Abbott was *predisposed* to kill anyone who aggressed upon him, either with actual or threatened violence.

There is no need to argue the invalidity of Larsen's testimony and the Prosecutor's charge of Murder. The jury disposed of this when Abbott was acquitted of Murder.

It was Abbott's opinion mid-trial that if it were true that Adan thought he wanted to use the restroom (and was escorting him outside to urinate and was guarding his privacy), *then* Abbott had to have been suffering from an "emotional disturbance" at the time to so misinterpret the situation. The jury dismissed it as a baseless hypothesis.

Before his trial, Abbott was not tested by a psychologist and a defense of incompetence was never further from his mind.

The wound Adan sustained penetrated his heart in a straight line, entering through the right ventricle, passing through the interventricular septum, and ending within the left ventricle. The wound was precisely one inch wide at the surface, tapering to a quarter of an inch inside. The wound was three and a half inches deep. Adan and Abbott were both in motion at the moment the wound was sustained. The sheer precision of the wound is the best argument that it was accidental. If a man slugs another man so that he hits his temple at exactly the right angle, killing him instantly, the *proof* it was an accident lies in the improbability of the exactitude of the blow to the temple. Under those conditions, not even a surgeon could have delivered a wound as precise as the wound Adan sustained.

Adan was stabbed only once. He sustained a few minor abrasions on his face when he fell to the sidewalk. Adan was walking backward through pedestrian traffic on Second Avenue. As Abbott and the crowd gathered around Adan when he collapsed, there was immediately a call to send for an ambulance. One man ran across the street to use a telephone, and Larsen ran up the street for the same purpose. Abbott did not leave Adan dying on the sidewalk, without concern. Once he was sure everything possible had been done to help Adan, he went to the door of the café and called Susan and Veronique. They came out. Fohsta rushed up to Abbott and asked him if he had seen what happened. Abbott replied, "Stay back from me," as he and the women were moving toward the corner. After Abbott threw down the knife and fled, Susan and Veronique returned to the café. They refused to speak to the police except in the presence of lawyers. They refused to identify Abbott. It was two days before the police could interrogate them. By then, the police had identified Abbott.

* * *

The trial lasted seven days, two hours each day. Abbott was tried in the largest courtroom in Manhattan. Half the seats were reserved for the press (more than seventy seats). It was arranged that no spectator saw the whole trial from start to finish (except for Jean Malaquais, a French philosopher and one of Abbott's friends). Mailer only attended the last two days of the trial. Guards turned people away who had been there two or three days in a row. The jury deliberated for two days.

—Naomi Zack, Ph.D.

PART THREE

Men of Letters

The breathless haste with which Americans work is spreading a lack of spirituality like a blanket. Even now one is ashamed of resting and pro-longed reflection almost gives people a bad conscience. Hours in which honesty is permitted have become rare and when they arrive, one is tired and does not merely want to "let oneself go" but one actually wishes to stretch out as long and wide and ungainly as one happens to be.

This is how people write letters and the style and the spirit of letters will always be a true "sign of the times."

— Nietzsche

Dear Lionel,

I read your piece "Koestler Pardon" in *The New Republic* and I cannot resist a comment on it. I am not displeased with Koestler's writings but it seems to me he had a nasty streak in his character. You no doubt referred to it when you distinguished Rosa Luxemburg's qualities he never had. But at any rate, I did like the old goat.

Because, as you said, he perceived a great truth in *Darkness At Noon* at a time no one else had any real idea what was going on. Even today the Marxists look at Nicolai Bukharin's trial externally, as if all he needed were a good lawyer. Bukharin was committed to the concept of "objective enemies," no matter their intentions.

All that needed to be done was to convince Bukharin that his political line was counterrevolutionary, and his theory of propaganda would lead him to the conclusion that he should cooperate with all accusations against him: blacken himself. Bukharin himself had (earlier) used this same "logic" in joining with Stalin in his attack on Trotsky. So he was only submitting to the law he himself upheld.

This is what became of Leninist "self-criticism."

A wise man once said the most dangerous threat to a nation or to an individual is to be convinced he is guilty of sins he is not guilty of. To burden his conscience with crimes unjustly, crimes he has never committed, is one of the darkest secrets of the human soul: *He is driven by his conscience to commit the crimes in reality,* so that he might have a chance of redeeming himself. This has been of some consolation to me. This is why I cannot accede to a share of guilt, where it does not have reality, in the events that resulted in my trial. Others must accede to me on this. When something has been completely misunderstood, the misunderstanding can never be completely removed.

Because when a man has been convinced he is guilty of sins he is innocent of, there is no other chance of getting rid of his consciousness of guilt. The doer and the deed must come together, and I refuse to make a criminal of myself.

This is how innocent men become "sinners" (criminals).

It was in the latter part of the year 1977 that I first wrote to Norman Mailer. As of this writing, that was about nine years ago. I remember the circumstances and where I was. I was at the federal prison in Butner, North Carolina. I was in solitary, handcuffed to the steel bedpost in my cell. I was waiting to be taken to the Medical Center in Missouri for major surgery. My gall bladder had been injured. I was waiting, handcuffed to my bed, for several months. Then I was taken by slow circuit on prison buses to the Medical Center. The doctor who ordered it was told that I was too dangerous to be flown there by airplane, which is the normal procedure for medical cases as serious as mine. It took several months to get me there once I was placed on a bus out of Butner. When I arrived, I was sent to Building Ten. This is where inmates are sent who are not brought there for surgery. It is punitive solitary confinement. Inmates sent to the Medical Center for surgery are always placed in Building One. I was ill but I was held in Building Ten because there was an unnamed inmate in Building One who said he was afraid of me. At least that is what the warden of the Medical Center told the federal judge after I'd finally complained in a letter. The federal judge, as soon as he'd received my letter, ordered the Warden to place me in Building One. I was carried over in a stretcher and examined that day by a doctor who immediately had me taken into emergency surgery and removed my gall bladder. It took me a month to recover. I was kept in a hospital cell during the recovery. There were complications and my liver was infected. As a result I contracted Australian hepatitis.

Then I was sent on the prison bus circuit to Lompoc Federal Prison in California. This took several months. Through all this I was writing letters to Norman Mailer about the Utah State Prison and how violence is inculcated in prisoners. None of the letters were about me or my life. Nor were they about Gary Gilmore, who was the subject of a book Mailer was writing. (Gilmore was executed in the Utah State Prison.) Over this period all inmates in federal prisons were allowed to seal their letters. It was an experiment that lasted just over two years and was the result of a lawsuit that I and about thirty others filed against the Bureau of Prisons in Washington, D.C., in 1972.

Just after I arrived at Lompoc—about the middle of 1978—I wrote Mailer and I told him I felt I had exhausted all I had to say about prisons and the inculcation of violence. We had been corresponding for about a year by then. I told him that someday, perhaps, he might write a letter for me. I meant to end our correspondence. But he wrote me and asked me to tell him about myself.

I responded, apologizing for not having done so in my letters. I told him everything about myself in one short letter. I am not sure what I told him in the letter, but it was vital statistics mainly. I ended it by telling him good-bye forever. But he wrote me again, insisting that I could be a writer, and he asked me my feelings about literature. I told him I did not want to be a writer because I revered literature and the world did not need another mediocre writer. I wrote him about literature I had read. Somehow I began thinking about myself and my life analytically. But I never wrote him about my life. I wrote him about my thoughts. There is a difference. I was shy of the empirical facts of my experience of life around me. As a Marxist, I had taught myself not to be deceived by empirical facts.

I had a difficult time with syntax. I felt deeply compromised by my experience. I felt that if I stood aside from my surroundings I would condemn everyone unjustly. So I took a share of it all on myself, not an unnatural thing for someone who has been too long in prison. It is a classic problem (I have since learned) all writers struggle with in getting their sea-legs.

I got into the habit of writing Mailer about everything under the sun. Because I could seal my letters, I felt free. Writing freely started a lot of subjective mental activity. I began to explore my feelings. It was not until I had arrived at Lompoc, after my letters on prison were finished, that I first mentioned to Mailer that I was a Marxist-Leninist. None of the prison letters were political in nature. Nor did any of those letters make reference to literature (or thinkers in any context).

Then the experiment came to a sudden end in June 1979. We could no longer seal our letters. There was a workstrike and I was transferred to Marion Federal Prison for allegedly inciting the strike. The strike demand was against the censorship of outgoing letters from prison. The strike lasted about a week. We did not win.

Early in 1980, after I'd spent a year in Marion Prison, Mailer told me that he thought that once I saw myself published I would accept that I was a writer. He marked out some passages from a few of my letters. His secretary typed them and sent them to me for my approval. I approved them and returned them. A literary agent sent the writings to *The New York Review of Books*. I had never heard of *The New York Review of Books*. My writings were accepted and published. A month later a contract to write a book about "life in prison" was sent me from a publishing house. Mailer had agreed to write an introduction. My circumstances in Marion Prison were not amenable to writing a book. I was in the midst of an endless series of hungerstrikes, rebellions, and murders. Marion Prison is small and has never held more than three hundred and fifty inmates. But it is always as explosive as a vial of nitroglycerin.

After we discussed the situation and I agreed that I could at least take material from my letters to Mailer and construct a book, I signed the contract. Then a lawyer sent me copies of my letters to Mailer. The letters had been arranged in chronological order. To my surprise, the earliest letter was the first letter I had written Mailer when I arrived at Lompoc Prison.

This is where the difficulties began, because, by the time I had arrived at Lompoc, I was through writing about prison. I had always been clear that I could not write about my personal life. I asked that my letters about prison be sent to me.

Mailer's secretary replied, telling me those letters had been lost. It was difficult to accept this, since the writings published in *The New York Review of Books* came directly from those letters. I knew prison literature and those letters stood as the most thorough examination of prisons written by anyone. After a series of disagreements, I quit communicating with Mailer's secretary over this and came into direct contact with a my editor, Erroll McDonald.

I was anxious now. I did not want to violate the contract, and (on top of this) my circumstances were such that there was every reason to believe I might not survive. Inmates were being baited and pitted against each other on an intense scale. All Marion inmates were there because they were violent and uncontrollable in other prisons and had been sent there from state prisons as well as federal prisons. Most of them had recently murdered other inmates in other prisons. These were the class of inmates famous for rehabilitating revolutionaries through nothing more than the sheer force of circumstances. Every assault, murder, or other crime by inmates was punished by federal prosecution in a local federal court. Almost every Marion inmate had so long a prison sentence that he did not care about being prosecuted again. The prisoners allowed the authorities to use them against each other to assault and murder each other.

After a series of communications with Mailer and Erroll McDonald, we arrived at the following solution: I would try to recall the lost prison letters and re-write them for the book manuscript. While the book could explain my circumstances, it would not be about my life in particular. It would merely encapsulate my reflections. It would be "life in prison" generally speaking. A series of meditations. Once, at Lompoc, I had attempted to write an autobiography and failed. I had given up trying—mainly because I lacked information and any idea of how to organize what I was doing. Experts have told me (including you) that my main problem was genre. As for the letters returned to me by Mailer's secretary, I would glean as much from them as I could and expand on them as needed. There was no need for chronological order (or letters from Mailer). This is how, for example, at the end of the book I came to quote from a letter written to Mailer from Lompoc, telling him I had received a parole date. That letter was written in late 1978.

The letters dated from Lompoc covered almost a two-year period. There were altogether just over seven hundred pages. Reduced to typed sheets, there would have been about four pages to a sheet—or about one hundred and seventy-five typed pages.

I read through all the letters and began thematically categorizing passages and omitting others until I had narrowed them to the fewest categories possible. These categories became the chapters. I rewrote about two-thirds of what finally became the finished product. The whole process, once I began, took only two weeks. I sent the completed manuscript and a list of possible book titles for the editor to choose from to the publisher. The editor, using his own judgment, omitted contradictory passages. He changed all the titles of the chapters. He rearranged the sequences of a few passages where he felt it was necessary. I have a copy of my original handwritten manuscript. The editor did not add chapters or take any chapters away. He did not add even a word. He took one passage and made it the book's preface—a passage where the phrase "second Adam" appears. He rejected all my title suggestions and titled the book *The Second Adam.*

Altogether, the editor could not have omitted more than about ten of my handwritten pages of contradictory passages. When I saw the typewritten edited manuscript, I did not have time to read it. I merely noted and approved the chapter titles. I struck out his title and titled it *In the Belly of the Beast.* I did not want it to be understood as an autobiography. At the peak of the "prison movement" in the early seventies, prisoners signed their letters to the underground prison reform press with this message. I wanted it to speak for all of *those* prisoners.

I gave Erroll McDonald credit for work he did not do because I thought it would help his career. I exaggerated the work he did.

I liked young Erroll.

But here is where the second large problem began: No one saw the manuscript and Erroll was not an intellectual. No one saw it until it was set in the first galley editions. The first galley editions were printed and then were automatically sent to all the major reviewers in America and Europe directly from the production room at the publishing house. I am sure this will never happen again to anyone. I was later told that only prison stories had been expected.

Norman Mailer (and everyone else) opened the galley edition and read it for the first time, at the same time all the reviewers were opening it and reading it all across America and Europe.

I was sent the galleys only after Mailer wrote the introduction. His introduction was still in manuscript and not in galleys.

Print has a way of objectifying thoughts and maximizing their power, as all writers know. It gives thought a life of its own. It really is analogous to conceiving offspring. I sadly recognized myself in print the way I guess a man recognizes himself in his bastard child. There was a conflict of emotions of pride and shame. It is not like this in any other medium—except if it be that of an actor's relation to the finished film in which he has acted a role. He must see himself like this secretly on screen—but he is protected outwardly by the category of "actor," since only an idiot would confuse him with the character in his role. (There are droves of such idiots, too.) Writers are not so fortunate. I knew I was in serious trouble.

The mere fact that Mailer's introduction was in manuscript form told me he had not seen and approved my manuscript. Both Mailer and McDonald later confirmed this.

For a writer, context is something he never wants to lose control of. He does not want what he writes to lose its context or to be placed in some other context. In my efforts to use syntax to resolve the problem between what is existential and its universal meanings, I had become a cipher easily translatable into a variety of contexts. I compromised myself even more in my book than circumstances had forced me.

Before I was taken out of Marion Prison (and before the galley edition of my book was printed), I wrote a book review for a literary journal, and I had begun writing to one of the editors about literature. With Sartre's *The Words* in mind, I wrote several letters about how I learned certain concepts *before* recognizing the thing the concepts referred to. These letters were about my first readings of Freud's monographs (when I was fourteen or fifteen years old) from books taken from an office in one of the buildings of the State Industrial School for Boys. I was intensely interested in the Freudian school for years afterward. I was explaining, through several examples, my surprise as a youth to learn that my attitude toward an idea acquired from reading seldom conformed with its realization when it was identified with the reality.

Just after the first galley editions of my book were distributed, selections of passages from those letters were published by one of the editors as a single reflection under the title "On Women." I had no idea anything was being published. When I opened the pages and saw it for the first time, I was surprised and pleased although it was not clear that I was writing about the intellectual befuddlements of a fifteen-year-old scholar in a juvenile penal institution. It was not clear that the subject of the writing was *semantics* (and not women). It was with the same pride and shame I read this. The writing was stylistically superb and, all things considered, it richly deserved to be published at the time. It was published opposite Norman Mailer's introduction to my book, printed first in the journal as an advance notice to the publication of *In the Belly of the Beast*. Just after "On Women" was published, I received a request to consider writing a piece on women's emancipation for *Vogue* magazine. *Vogue* reviewed my book favorably.

Norman Mailer's introduction seemed slightly loaded with the normal amount of small inaccuracies anyone commits in the course of recommending someone to skeptical readers. Most of them were political inaccuracies but the only inaccuracy that irritated me enough to correct, however, involved my book's chilling description of a murder. I have called it in my play "The Killer Vignette." In his introduction, Mailer accidentally identified this with me, as something I had done and been convicted of and sentenced for in court. In several letters, I had previously gone to some lengths explaining to him an incident in prison that took place when I was twenty-one years old in which a forty-two-year-old inmate died ten days after he and his friend (who was thirty-five years old) were wounded in an assault on me in the center hall of the Utah State Prison. It was worlds removed from "The Killer Vignette."

It was a mistake made in haste, of course, but it piqued me nonetheless. To be truthful, it appalled me, and so I wrote in the margin of the manuscript of his introduction: "Remove this; it is not what I was convicted of." No doubt for the same reasons that the error was made, my witticism was overlooked. I meant to call attention to it and further jolt the imagination (playfully) at the same time by not *denying* the monstrosity. But the passage was not removed from his introduction. Erroll McDonald overlooked my correction and it was printed in the first editions of *In the Belly of the Beast*. When I saw it printed in the journal, I also wrote the editor about this matter of Mailer's introduction.

"The Killer Vignette" was a synthesis—a universal emblem of prison murder. The psychology of it was suggested to me by the novel *Juggler* in which the author had displayed unprecedented psychological insight. I had empathized with the emblem when I wrote and it had sickened me. "The Killer Vignette" was so realistic I almost had to wonder if the police could question me over this.

The error was removed from Mailer's introduction only in later editions of the book and has never appeared in the paperback editions of *In the Belly of the Beast,* although in thirteen foreign translations of my book that error has never been removed.

But this was how things stood when I arrived in Manhattan.

I arrived in Manhattan with the intention of seeking a way to emigrate from America. My commitment to my federal parole would have been completed in 1986. I planned to seek a way to shorten this period and leave as soon as possible.

In the meantime, I planned to prepare myself while I supported myself as a writer. I would live quietly and pursue my purposes. This was understood by everyone.

I had declined appearing on the television program "Good Morning America," but I was told that Mailer had committed himself and would appear even if I refused to do so. It was for this reason I changed my mind and appeared for a few minutes on "Good Morning America." I declined interviews (which the publishing house arranged) but submitted to two of the interviews for reasons similar to why I made the television appearance. I asked the publishing house not to release the address of the halfway house where I was staying because I did not want news reporters seeking me out there.

I understood the Freudian attitude that would rise up in response to my Marxist attitude. I understood almost perfectly what the public would have to do with me. I had denounced my country in ways and in terms it had never been denounced before.

I knew (as I know today) that those who met me and spent time with me genuinely liked me as a person. I also know I was not what they expected. They expected a "personality," with all the vulnerabilities of personalities.

I was pleasantly disappointed myself since I too had preconceptions about them. All the responsible people I met and spent time with I liked instantly. They were intellectually alive in the world in ways no mere academics could ever be. They were my spiritual brothers. I have not been disappointed in that pleasure, for not one of them has commented about me publicly in the press.

I attended only one dinner party and that at a small restaurant in the West Village. I invited a Polish emigrant, who had written a book about a boy caught in the hurricane of the Second World War in east Central Europe. I wanted to be his friend and to learn what he could tell me about Poland and its present occupation. They tell me he was never so talkative as he was with me at the table that evening. In addition to him, my suspicious but charming publisher, Mailer, and the editor of what I took to be a small literary review, were present (as well as three of their employees and two of their friends). It could not have lasted more than an hour. I arrived in a taxi alone and I walked back to the halfway house alone.

The McDowell Colony is the strictest place of its kind. All contact with the outside world is broken. On request, a writer can be locked in his room and take his meals there. At McDowell I would have been spared that special kind of destruction that was gathering strength while I was at the halfway house. Everyone was trying to have me placed in McDowell and I was touched. I understood.

I was at the halfway house for exactly six weeks. It was on a Sunday, just as dawn was rising, that I became a fugitive.

In the Belly of the Beast was an unfortunate caesarean birth but I cannot regret its mongoloid blessedness or its multitude of blemishes, even though it may eventually destroy me. It has made me stronger.

My mind was imbued with my study of Nietzsche's *The Birth of Tragedy* at the time I composed the play for publication. It was coincidental, because I was avidly thinking out those cultural problems when the proposal to publish it was made. As a youth, I had read *The Birth of Tragedy* and, for lack of knowledge, had totally misunderstood it. With the keys of new knowledge in my hand, I had been for months on end opening the vaults of every sphinx that stood before all I had previously thought I knew just as well as anyone else. I went back to everything I had read and rediscovered it anew.

The last word Nietzsche wrote about *The Birth of Tragedy* was written in his last book, *Ecce Homo*. In *Ecce Home* Nietzsche wrote a short retrospective account of each of his published works in the chapter titled "Why I Write Such Good Books." Each retrospective was a few pages in length. *Ecce Homo* itself was only about a hundred pages in length.

His retrospective on *The Birth of Tragedy* was divided into four reflections.

Nietzsche devoted the first reflection to the *title* he had given to his first book, *The Birth of Tragedy*.

Nietzsche regretted the title he had given it. Nietzsche was a young man when it was published in 1872. He was, at the time, a follower of Richard Wagner. Richard Wagner was a virulent anti-Semite and stood (with Dostoevsky) at the beginning of *modern* anti-Semitism—the earlier anti-Semitism being centered around religious objections to the Jews. Richard Wagner wrote a book accusing the Jews of a lack of aesthetic sensitivity and he accused the Jews of destroying culture. Richard Wagner was a political radical, a revolutionary partisan of German nationalism.

In Wagner's operas and symphonies, young Nietzsche envisioned a regeneration of German culture to a *higher* cultural level. Nietzsche was still a boy and not cognizant of the dark struggle against Jewish intellectuals that pervaded non-Jewish European *intellectual traditions* in nineteenth-century Europe, which were an historical outgrowth of Christian schools and universities.

Wagner's music was visibly causing social change in Germany but young Nietzsche was politically naive and did not understand its reactionary nature, which was a regression to a *lower* period of German culture.

The birth of tragedy out of the spirit of music was Nietzsche's formula for the phenomenon of Wagner's impact on German culture, which was nationalistic through and through, and confirmed Plato's theory that music had the power to destroy or change social institutions.

His essay was timely and was written to explain the greatness of Richard Wagner's genius. It was Richard Wagner who, in young Nietzsche's mind, was fathering "the birth of tragedy" in Germany—as it was once fathered in ancient Greece, where it called forth Greek culture as we think we know it today. Nietzsche envisioned a Germany as graceful as ancient Greece—where society placed its greatest value on friendship between its citizens, and civil and criminal courts virtually did not exist for the arbitration of complaints.

"To be fair to *The Birth of Tragedy,*" Nietzsche wrote, "one has to forget a few things. Its effect and fascination were due to what was wrong with it—its practical application to Wagnerism, as if that were a symptom of *ascent.* In this respect, this essay was an event in the life of Wagner: It was only from that moment on that Wagner's name elicited high hopes. People still remind me of this today. . . ."

Nietzsche had subtitled *The Birth of Tragedy:* "The Re-Birth of Tragedy out of the Spirit of Music." When he later saw the book cited by this subtitle, he wrote that ". . . what people had ears for was only a new formula for the art, the intentions, the task of Wagner."

Of the title *The Birth of Tragedy,* Nietzsche's last word was that "Hellenism and Pessimism" would have been a less ambiguous title. Nietzsche's last word on the subject was that it was indifferent to politics. Only if it is viewed with neutrality does *The Birth of Tragedy* seem to be untimely, wrote Nietzsche.

When Nietzsche discovered Wagner's anti-Semitic writings, he began to revolt.

Paul Ree, a Jewish psychologist, had written a book dealing with moral sensitivity, and Nietzsche read it with profit. He and Paul Ree became friends and Nietzsche made a violent and noisy break with Richard Wagner and the non-Jewish intellectual tradition of Europe. His next work, just weeks after this, was *Human, All Too Human.*

In his second retrospective reflection on *The Birth of Tragedy* (in *Ecce Homo*), Nietzsche writes that his beginning as a thinker with *The Birth of Tragedy* was "exceedingly strange" because as a *thinker* Nietzsche found the parallel for his own "inmost experience" in his instincts *against* rationality. Through his meditations in *The Birth of Tragedy* he discovered this parallel in the *Dionysian*—Dionysus as opposed to Socrates, whom Nietzsche saw as representing the decay of Greek culture. He discovered that morality itself was a *symptom* of decadence, i.e., a sure sign that morality did not have real existence. Christians live as though aspects of existence can be repudiated and subtracted, but it is precisely these aspects of existence that are on an infinitely higher plane in the order of human values. And Nietzsche wrote that in the Dionysian is the formula for the highest affirmation of existence; ". . . A Yes-saying without reservation, even to suffering, even to guilt, even to what is questionable and strange in existence." This formula takes life's expectations beyond categories of pessimism and optimism. Nietzsche repudiated all moral judgment of existence. This eventually led to his great work, *The Genealogy of Morals.*

His third retrospective reflection begins with a summary remark on the concept of the tragic. Elsewhere he had identified it with the love of fate and here he summarized it as life rejoicing over its own inexhaustibility, even in the sacrifice of its highest types. Nietzsche repudiated the concept of *evil* in the fate of man and in the understanding of the movements of tragedy. This he called Dionysian and he understood it as the bridge to the psychology of the tragic poet. Tragedy is then not the catharsis of emotions of pity and terror before suffering and pain (as Christians and Aristotle understood it) but to be oneself *beyond* all terror and pity and to be the eternal joy of becoming.

Nietzsche then went straight to the heart of the matter and brought into view what was lacking: tragic wisdom. He wrote that in the sense that he alone had repudiated the pessimistic experience of tragedy, he had the right to consider himself the first tragic philosopher:

Before me this transposition of the Dionysian into a philosophical pathos did not exist: *tragic wisdom* was lacking. I have looked in vain for signs of it even among the *great* Greeks in philosophy, those of the two centuries before Socrates.

How does one affirm and welcome every aspect of existence; how does one move beyond all pity and fear before suffering and destruction? What wisdom can grow out of the affirmation of the aspects of existence that leave us destroyed or maimed, except a radical repudiation of those aspects of existence in religions (such as Christianity)? How else but to posit the value and meaning of life in a dream-world after death? What is the basis of tragic wisdom?

Nietzsche's answer: "the doctrine of the eternal recurrence, that is, of the unconditional and infinitely repeated circular course of all things." This was the doctrine of Nietzsche's *Zarathustra,* and Nietzsche wrote that it *might* have been taught in antiquity by Heraclitus and he noted that the Stoa had traces of it, for the Stoics derived their main notions from Heraclitus.

In the fourth (and last) retrospective reflection on *The Birth of Tragedy,* Nietzsche draws on a theme raised in the introductory remarks to the chapter, that explains that no one can get more out of things than he already knows. He writes, "A psychologist might still add that what I heard as a young man listening to Wagnerian music really had nothing to do with Wagner and that when I described Dionysian music I described what only I had heard. . . ."

Therefore, Nietzsche recommended that wherever he wrote the name of Wagner in texts of that period (mainly his *Wagner in Bayreuth*), "one need not hesitate to put down my name or the word 'Zarathustra.'" Nietzsche wrote that he had *instinctively* transposed and transfigured everything he experienced into "the new spirit that I carried in me."

Nietzsche wrote of *The Birth of Tragedy,* "A tremendous hope speaks out of this essay" and he went on to predict: "I promise a tragic age: tragedy will be re-born when humanity has weathered the consciousness of the hardest but most necessary wars *without suffering from it.*" Nietzsche's last word on *The Birth of Tragedy* indicates clearly that Nietzsche was of the opinion that tragedy was dead and that "the birth of tragedy" had not, after all, come about through the genius of the man whom he idolized in his youth, Richard Wagner.

I do not mean to posture myself as someone who is lecturing you or telling you things you do not already know. My probably didactic style must be tedious to you, but I hope you will have patience and permit me to go on. My gift has also been a curse: I was born with excessive faculties for what psychologists call "empathy." At least one psychologist, who measured it on a metric scale, has reported that my capacity rose over the mean average so far that it went off the chart. It is normal to me to find it difficult to separate the feelings and emotions of others from my own. On average, I therefore have a confusion of experience and memory. As time has gone by, and I have grown older, I have become more and more aware of this. Thoughts can rise up exoterically as if from outside me. They can represent knowledge and experiences that are not mine. It is true that we only get out of reading no more than what we already know. This is at least one of the reasons that the sages lamented the day the Torah was translated into other tongues. They said on that day another Golden Calf was fashioned.

There is a word Nietzsche used which his best translator, Walter Kaufmann, renders as "selfish." This may well be the standard meaning of the German he wrote in. But I think the more proper meaning and translation should be "selfness." It is this that I acquire as time goes on.

There is also the distinction between wisdom and the intellectual faculties. Wisdom is prior to and furnishes the culture of the intelligence. Modern philosophy since the nineteenth century, for example, has exhibited more intellectual brilliance than wisdom.

Wisdom seems to me more deeply rooted in an individual's inborn response to life. It is also how a people responds to life. The accumulated treasures of the wisdom of a people seems to me to be expressed in its culture. How people treat one another and go about their lives, how they do things, what their habits and their values are, etc.—all of this is a product of wisdom. When people watch with interest an affair involving others unfold before their eyes, they understand it according to the *kind* of wisdom they have, in the same way they have their own bodies. It is not intellectual. Tragedy does not originate on a stage but in the world, where the real intercourse occurs. The kind of cruelty that came into existence by watching others suffer on the stage is a different kind of cruelty than that which came into existence by watching the suffering of others in the *world*.

All tragedy is a movement that converges on the one thing that happens to us all, the one event none of us can escape: Death and destruction awaits us all. A wise man lives in the house of mourning because he understands this. At least in western civilization, actual death is something which is kept carefully out of sight and out of mind. It is something unnatural, something theatrical at best, a diseased intrusion in human life. The anticipation of real death and destruction has become almost the only justification for violating what in our civilization passes itself off as virtues. The idea of living well is dwarfed and crooked in practice when it is confronted with the idea of dying well, which is the true subject and the sole edifying meaning of tragedy and its moments.

Holding separate and apart the stage from the world is similar to the religious practice of holding the world itself separate and apart from "heaven." Uniting the two must be no different from the return of thought to the body. Then, one could put *"mortido ergo sum"* in place of the ill-fated "I" (*ego*). The body in space, in its possibilities, is infinite.

The types of bodies are also calculable, observable. I have seen slaves standing in the shoes of princes and I have seen princes in the shoes of slaves. Probabilities (chance) placed them there, and chance pits itself against them as individuals who must struggle merely to exist. This is the human comedy that amuses the gods—what we humans at our best understand as tragedy. Fate has tricked us all and only a fool would be afraid to pick up the dice and roll them himself, to take up the game on a grand scale (and to its limits) and apply it to everything—to himself, to heaven and earth, to the "laws of nature" and the whole universe. To paraphrase a nineteenth-century argument still valid today: We can only think of the physical universe as a finite mass quantum, with an infinite number of centers of force. Any other conception is metaphysical and useless. Every combination of forces represents a transformation. The universe must therefore pass through a great but calculable number of transformations. Every possible transformation in infinite time would have already existed. It would have existed an infinite number of times already.

Between every transformation and its next recurrence, every other possible transformation would necessarily occur. Each transformation would condition the entire sequence of transformations in the same series. A recurrent movement of identical series is demonstrated: The universe describes a circular movement and has repeated itself an infinite number of times *in infinitum*. And because the universe has not reached a final state, mechanistic theory stands refuted and at best as only a provisional hypothesis.

All of this is coming back again. You, me, this book, this room, this moment and the next, this world and everything we think about it, will be destroyed and come back again. There is no reality more abundantly in evidence—even in scientific proofs—than that of repetition. Space is a curvature. The Hegelian dialectic must retrace its steps. Even the Big Bang theory postulates a Big Bang at the end.

What is generally called the theory of probabilities is absolutely self-evident, as self-evident as the fact that $1+1=2$. *It is probable* that the general theory of probabilities has its self-evidence in the most fundamental and inherent impulses of all forms of life. I see no other way any living organism can move through existence. It is the drive for the eternal recurrence. Theoreticians have attempted to dismiss the reality of the general theory of probabilities in the same way David Hume dismissed the reality of causality. This is as superficial, when carried to extremes, as denying that bodies in space exist.

What is called "the doctrine of the eternal recurrence" the Temple priesthood in ancient Jerusalem called "the teaching of the circle." I believe the cycles we sense in the Torah were understood only on the basis of the teaching of this wisdom. The evaluations of the sacrifices, the import of the festivals, the worship of "the One who sitteth above the circle"—I believe it was partially expressed in the wisdom of *Koheleth*.

Solomon's teacher was Zadok. Zadok was the hereditary founder of the Sadducee High Priesthood in the Temple of the One G-d in Jerusalem. The authentic Sadducees were blood descendants of Zadok. What little we know of the knowledge imparted in "the teaching of the circle" we barely sense today in the Jerusalem Talmud and the Zohar (and other cabbala works). It was through this knowledge that the full meaning and secrets of the Torah were imparted. Those who barely knew of it exoterically (and at a distance) speak of the priests "casting lots"* in the latter

---

*The readings were taken from a board. I see its precursor in the legendary "alphabet of creation," which hands down as the wisdom of Father Abraham—which we also barely sense in the taoist *feng-shui* reckoning board, whose antecedents in the oracle-bones appear in the ten Heavenly Stems and twelve Earthly Branches. This reckoning device must have originally been a scientific instrument and it could not have *originated* in China. The board measured the changes of states and movements of at least two forces, magnetic and gravitational. It was imported to China probably from the Mesopotamian civilization. The twenty-two pictographs of the "stems and branches" (*kan* and *chih*), however little they resemble the Semitic alphabet, probably came from the same source the twenty-two letters of the Hebrew alphabet originally came from. I am aware of the linguistic arguments against this. They are unsound for a variety of reasons, not least of which is the refusal to contemplate the distinctions between pictographs (seeing and touching) and phonetics (hearing and speaking).

The taoist temples were seven stories high and in architectural specification resembled the tower-temples of Mesopotamia. Even the word "tao" (which means "teaching") resembles how a Chinese would say "torah" (which also means "teaching"). The descriptions of directions and forces in the cabbala (especially the *bereshith* of the Zohar) resemble in mode the old understanding of the movements of the lines of the *I Ching*. The taoist Diagram of the Supreme

period of the Wars of the Priests.

Koheleth set judgment in the land and this form of judgment was practiced by all the people throughout the land. This is how law was applied. I think the practice of this wisdom was spread to what became ancient Greece by the Phoenicians and Hebrews in the reign of Solomon. This is why staged tragedy (and that peculiar kind of cruelty) appeared in most ancient Greece, because the wisdom was lost and cut off from its roots after Solomon died and Judah became a separate kingdom. All that remained was the isolated form of theatrical tragedy estranged from its understanding. *Koheleth* embodies the epitome of tragic wisdom: How and why does man suffer?

When Israel, even "from Dan to Asher," exists again in peace, without war and secure, tragic wisdom must come back.

I am aware that the *Koheleth* has been fixed by experts as originating in Persia because of the internal evidence of a few words of Persian origin. The same thing is said about the Torah. No one doubts today that Zarathustra was at the bottom of the origin of Persia itself.

So far as the origins of *Koheleth* are concerned (not to mention the Torah), I think the experts should concern themselves more with the subject of how scrolls were reproduced in the ancient world. The Persian words were more probably the work of ambitious copyists, eager to correct the scribes.

As always,
Jack

Dear Robert W.

I never meant to say Spartacus did not have ideas about what he was doing. His ideas, however, were (I think) contingent on how he expected the Germanic tribes to behave.

Pole is almost identical, even in detail, to the ten *sefirah* of the cabbalistic *Sefer Ha-Temunah*. These are but a few of the welter of identities which must compel the conclusion that earliest Chinese civilization was derived from Mesopotamia. Abraham and his family were hereditary priests in the Temple of Sin in Haran, a Mesopotamian city. Sin was the moon-goddess who mediated between earth and the One G-d. (The word "sin" is no doubt descended from practices which occurred in the worship of Sin.)

The Roman armies kept blocking his progress toward the north. He was not a revolutionary trying to found a society.

At that time in Roman history Italy was suffering a long series of raids by large bands of Germanic tribes seeking nothing more than plunder. Spartacus was, in relation to the Germans, carrying out a rearguard action against the Roman Empire.

But the most important revolt was the so-called "Servile War" (or the First Slave War) in Sicily. They were mostly semitic slaves, from Syria. They, unlike Spartacus (a Thracian, leading mostly Celts and Germans) tried to found a nation and govern themselves on the island of Sicily.

A Syrian slave named Eunus ("the benevolent") organized and led this revolt. It lasted about three years and stirred up all the slaves in the Roman Empire, including those in southern Italy and even in the possessions in and around the Aegean Sea (the mines, Patmos among them).

When it was crushed, a new slave revolt erupted thirty years later (circa 100 B.C.E.).

Eunus was much more interesting than Spartacus, in every way. He stands at the beginning of the resistance of slaves against Rome. While Eunus and the slaves of Sicily were fighting the Roman army, the conflict over the Temple was at its peak. It was over this same period the Dead Sea book-rolls were being written and the Qumran sect had taken occupation of the caves along the Dead Sea. The main sects developed in Judea over this period as well.

—But this revolt in Sicily set a pattern, not just in Sicilian history but of the revolts in general. It seems certain it was signaled by waves of invasions into Italy from the north, by the Germanic tribes. Almost an allied action.

Each of these slave wars was about thirty years apart: First Slave War, 135 B.C.E.; Second Slave War, 100 B.C.E. After this second slave war in Sicily, the next one was led by Spartacus—again, about thirty years later (circa 73 B.C.E.). This means each generation raised a war against Rome from within.

I think Spartacus changed his notions about himself and what he was doing many times. But the *constant* must have always been the idea of the Germanic tribes invading the Italian peninsula. This overweening optimism was his tragedy. He finally must have pinned all his hopes on that. I think, because of his military behavior, that Spartacus felt that if he engaged Rome at certain moments and places—and drew Roman troops away from the northern frontier—the Germanic tribes would perceive it and invade across a weakened frontier, attacking the Romans while they were divided and moving apart.

It was a pipedream. Spartacus and his gladiators were probably men with "heroic" ideas about themselves (these men who killed each other on command of their masters!).

Eunus is interesting for many reasons. The "sacred fish" at the sanctuary of Syracuse was taken up by Eunus and his followers as a sacred symbol. And it later became the symbol of Christianity for slaves. Also (among other reasons Eunus was interesting) the insurrectionary government in Sicily lasted for three years and shook the foundations of the Roman Empire. Whatever Eunus was doing it had the support of slaves everywhere in the Roman Empire.

Out of the ashes of his defeat, endless small rebellions started everywhere and it created at least two major slave wars.

After Spartacus was defeated, however, there never again was a slave war against Rome.

Diodorus reports (as do other ancient sources as well) that the small farmers and proletariat were class conscious of themselves yet took up a *third* position in their attitude toward the insurrectionary power based in Enna (almost the exact geographical center of Sicily).

The free workers and farmers rejoiced at the destruction of the wealthy and carried on plunder (stealing, vengeance). Yet they then denounced the slaves, blaming them for these actions, to the Roman police.

They betrayed both the *latifundia* owners and the rebel slaves. In fact it is suggested they helped the Roman armies by passing them information spied out on the strength and position of the rebel slaves. Yet the slaves would not harm them.

The behavior of the proletariat toward slave revolts throughout history seems to defy "Marxist optimism," Marxist theory. It seems to be a history of betrayal.

—The Germanic tribes would sweep down from the north, plunder, burn, and destroy, and then escape back up into the steppes. Spartacus never *grasped* that they fought like freebooters.

The slaves never succeeded in their revolts because they had no moral values higher than those of their Roman masters (stoicism was the highest expression of Roman values). The slaves could not found a society for that reason. It was only when Rome laid its claws on the Judeans and the Judeans revolted that Rome began to die as a way of life.

The value of Judean money was based on the worth of just men and was regulated by the Temple. The value of Roman money was based on subjection, conquest: value in *things* (slaves, cattle, land). It was fixed in actual *things.*

It was (ultimately) the influence of the more valuable Judean currency that liquidated Roman wealth and made it unprofitable to keep slaves. That is how the slaves of Rome eventually were set free.

It *was* a revolt in values against Rome, a revolt in morality.

—My study of the origins of values reaches into antiquity and has called into question many of the crucial dogmas central to Marxism. Rome was "dead and stinking" long before the Germans began winning major battles, long before they sacked Rome. Indeed, it was a Judean who opened the gates of Rome for the Germans when they finally arrived.

The laws that govern the circulation of money are creative and only formulated *post hoc:* The laws of the state are developed after the fact of the existence of forms of liquidation and exchange.

All of our laws of arithmetic are reflections in consciousness of money relations and circulation. It is *money* that was the creative element; which organized means of production.

Judged from *any* standpoint, liquid wealth represents the constant improvement of values—as well as the constant amelioration of the condition of society.

It was the circulation of money with which the ancient Akkadians (Sargon the Great) overthrew the tyranny of the Sumerian civilization and the circulation of money that formed the basis of *reason* in human affairs. This is why the Hammurabi Code so resembled the laws of Moses handed down in Sinai later.

Were I to guess I would assert that the dream of wealth, at its essence, is the urge to return to Eden, to re-create the original condition of man.

* * *

While the Spartacus Rebellion was underway, the War of the Priests was at its highest pitch. The usurpers, who had taken over the Sadducee Priesthood—the High Priesthood—by killing and exiling the authentic, hereditary core of the Sadducees, had barricaded themselves in the walled Temple precinct and were under siege by the Judaic Pharisees. Onias the Righteous, said to be one of the last of the authentic hereditary descendants of Zadok still alive in Judea, was brought up by the Pharisees to the walls of the Temple and was asked to talk the usurpers into surrendering. Onias (meaning "The Circle Drawer") instead delivered a speech on "brotherly love" and asked both sides to live in peace. He was instantly stoned to death where he stood by the Pharisee forces (for his treachery). Onias had a reputation among the poor and ignorant for being able to cause rain. His death angered them.

Onias later had his wishes fulfilled, in a Sanhedrin that subordinated the Pharisees to the wicked Idumean "Sadducee" High Priesthood—the same Sanhedrin that stooped to the low level of deciding cases in law that were outside of the caste jurisdiction of the High Priesthood—cases of Galilean peasants and fraudulent country preachers (all of whom felt the Temple had been desecrated but did not grasp how).

It was almost at the same time the "heroes" of Spartacus were being nailed to crosses (along the road from Capua to Rome) that the Roman general, Pompey, took sides with the Pharisees, stormed Jerusalem, and broke into the Temple, putting everyone to the sword. About twelve thousand Judeans were slaughtered in the affair altogether (circa 70 B.C.E.).

The *real* war over Rome began: The great Julius Caesar, having mastered the hunting-ground of the German tribes (i.e., the Gaul's) now turned toward Pompey (his last barrier to absolute supremacy over Rome) just as once Romulus confronted Remus for similar reasons and for the same prize.

The War of the Priests must have had its beginnings in the introduction of Hellenic culture throughout the known world. The Greeks extended friendship to little Judea in the time of Alexander the Great. Whatever the forms of conflict that preceded it, it resulted in a dispute over the duties of the priesthood, and three major sects arose. The Sadducees represented the blooded nobility in the High Priesthood and traced its tradition to a priest from Shiloh named Zadok, who is said to have been King Solomon's teacher. The Sadducees were the most learned of men and when they disputed within their caste over *mishnah* (temple law) they were noted for ideologically attacking each other with the savagery with which ordinary people might treat hostile strangers. A Sadducee had it in his blood to stand alone and account for himself. It was his instinct to scorn supporters.

Whatever the original cause of the conflict or the details of the disputes, it all revolved around a single question: Man's fate. (This is interesting because the Greeks were never able to discuss tragedy in any depth philosophically and fate was outside the scope of their understanding.)

The Sadducees held that when mankind and the world are destroyed, all that is good will be destroyed along with all that is bad. The Sadducees held that, although man could judge good and evil, there was no ultimate value in one or the other. The Sadducees could not and would not be the judges of the morals or righteousness of the common people. All of mankind shared a common fate with the earth and one another. They would exist and be destroyed eternally and nothing could change it.

The Pharisees held that the people who worshipped the One G-d at the Temple in Jerusalem were different—otherwise any religion, heathen and otherwise, was the same. And if that were so, of what relevance was the Priesthood and the House of G-d? The Pharisees argued that—because of the people who are righteous and loved the ways of the Torah, who came to the Temple in the proper times and seasons, who worshipped G-d with all their might—when the world and all mankind are destroyed the World to Come will be a more righteous world (*gan eden*). The Pharisees held that each individual would return and be what he made of himself in this world. The Pharisees believed the fate of the Jews was special.

The Essenes held that the world was evil. Of the three main sects, the Essenes alone were deeply influenced by Greek philosophy and the Zoroasterian religions. They believed the end of the world was upon them but they had no conception of the total destruction of the planet itself. They believed in a heaven and not in this earth G-d gave to Adam to maintain and care for. They thought the end of the world would be a war of the forces of light and righteousness against the forces of darkness and evil. They practiced celibacy, preached the end of the world, set up charity organizations for the poor, and prepared for war against Rome, which they took to be "Kittim" in the Book of Daniel. When the Essenes vanished overnight, the Zealots stood in their place in force. I would guess the whole Essene movement took the logical step at some point and became convinced that the moment of the war between the Sons of Light and the Sons of Darkness had *actually* begun. They became Zealots. Jesus Christ, in his speeches, reveals clearly that his *roots* were in the Essenes. The early Christian monastic practices were taken directly from the Essenes as well.

Josephus was a Judean official and he went over to the side of Rome against the Zealots. Josephus witnessed the destruction of Jerusalem and the Temple and the destruction of his people and their country. He was asked by a member of the Roman nobility to write the history of his people. Josephus lent credibility to the Essenes and the story of Jesus Christ so that the non-Jews might be sympathetic or at least tolerant of his people because, in the story, Jesus was a Judean. In a booklet Josephus wrote called "Against Apion" it is clear he was not a Christian and did not believe in Jesus. It was a strong defense of the Jews before the Roman senate.

It seems clear that the old Persian Zoroasterian faith was practiced in Arabia but it met resistance from a very ancient cultic religion involving idols—probably idols similar to those Laban used. These were household clan idols, not tribal idols (such as the Golden Calf was). These cults were involved in a kind of planet worship, a highly structured astrological metaphysics. The Zoroasterian religion, with its traditions of "holy war" (Zoroaster was the first to invent holy war as a form of religious asceticism), was probably forced by the sword on the Arab nations. And as the Persian power withdrew, the older cultic practices tried to re-emerge—but their power, of course, was gone. The influence of the Zoroasterian magi religion must have also been felt by the Zealots (who originated in Galilee): They too advocated "jihad" and, in attacking the Sadducees, declared no one was their master except God. Their revolt was against Rome and (as in the Maccabee Revolt) against the High Priesthood they felt had become an instrument of Roman domination.

The evidence of Graetz (and Josephus) suggests that when the Zealots were defeated decisively at Masada, the remnant fled into the Arabian desert and returned to the ancient homeland of the children of Shem. Mecca is the Arabic transliteration of "Mesha," and Zafar is the Arabic transliteration of "Sephar," located at the tip of the Arabian peninsula. Graetz reports that it was this remnant of Judeans (with their complaints against the Temple priesthood at Jerusalem) who taught the Arabian tribes the tradition that they were the children of Ishmael. It is ironic that when the Moslems swept the world they constructed a mosque over the remains of the Temple, which the Zealots once took possession of by force —which *originally* was the main reason the Roman soldiers destroyed it.

The word "Palestine" originated with the *Greeks,* who, led by Alexander, conquered everything as far east as the Indus River and into Egypt. Josephus and others mention the little kingdom of "Philistia" at the same time they use the term "Palestine" (Philistia was in Gaza). So the word "Palestine" did not derive from "Philistine," which had no Greek origin. Philistia is a semitic word.

The root of "Palestine" is the Greek *palestia,* which meant *strife,* wrestling. A *palestria* was a place set up for physical education in the art of wrestling. Another irony is that the Maccabees complained that not only did the Greeks set up a Temple to Apollo in Jerusalem, but also that the Greeks set up *palestrias* in the city and that even the priests, when their daily duties were fulfilled in the Temple, relaxed by exercising in the *palestrias.* It was part of the Greek art of friendship and it was for this reason Greeks never dueled. It was for reasons pertaining to the *palestrias* the Maccabees complained, because the Hellenic alliance was too strong and Hellenic culture was being forced on the Judeans. The suffix "-ine," attached to this root, must have designated the entire area of Judean lands. The Greeks were at first in admiration of the Judeans, and the Spartans of Greece claimed to have in their possession ancient documents that proved their ancestors were once Hebrews.

The Greeks (as with the Romans later) must not have understood the form of government the Judeans had. So they called their lands "the land of strife" (which is what "Palestine" would have meant in Greek). The irony is that the name of Israel was bestowed upon Father Jacob when he prevailed over an angel in a wrestling match that lasted all night and ended in friendship.

The Roman senate placed Herod as king over the tributary lands the Romans designated as the Palestine. Palestine had become a protectorate as a result of Pompey's intrusion into the War of the Priests, which ended in his bloody entrance into Jerusalem and his desecration of the Temple. Palestine was probably the most lucrative source of income and influence of all the nations within the Roman Empire. For this reason Herod was a powerful king. His army was composed mainly of mercenaries and freed slaves from other nations and nationalities in the Roman Empire and included ethnic Germans as well as Celts and Thracians. Herod acquired his army and employed it to conquer and gather back to the staff of Judah all the lands of all the tribes of Israel that had been lost in the war against Assyria over five hundred years before.

In the time of Herod those lands were separate kingdoms, and the Jews in those lands were minorities governed by foreign powers. Herod was allowed to do this in order to unite Palestine and to normalize the levy of taxes for Rome. Herod eventually recovered most of the lands, clear up to the Lebanon.

Herod built magnificent extensions to the Temple and carried out great maintenance works to restore its grandeur as Solomon originally constructed it. Herod was a great king, but he was hardly another Solomon, and it might be argued that it was his very ambition to model himself after Solomon that was the source of his tragedy. Herod was without blood and he knew it. As Herod moved toward his horrible end, the enmity of the people against Rome grew. When he died, the kingdom began to fall apart and the people were in open revolt against Rome to liberate their lands from foreign rule. No people in antiquity, especially under Rome, displayed more heroism and contempt for torture and death than the Judeans.

Outside Jerusalem today archeologists are uncovering huge "mass graves" which probably were a result of the eventual siege against Jerusalem that Rome conducted in its terrible war against the Judeans and that ended in the total destruction of the Temple and the city itself. Under the command of the Roman Emperor, Vespasian (his son) surrounded Jerusalem while the Judeans fortified it from within. Vespasian laid siege against Jerusalem for several months during which no one left or entered the city. Vespasian dug a huge trench along the outside of the walls around Jerusalem. The trench was about thirty feet deep. In defiance of the armies outside the walls the Judeans danced and sang on the walls and hurled insults at the Roman soldiers. As a final show of contempt for the Romans, the Judeans ran up the ramparts and hurled their bodies into the ranks of the soldiers on the ground—hundreds, perhaps thousands, died this way. By the time Vespasian's army breached the walls months later they were so enraged and insulted they could not contain themselves. The Temple precinct was like an inner city and it too was walled. In the War of the Priests, the Zealots had won and they were now confronting Rome on the steps of the Temple. The Roman soldiers had been ordered by the Emperor himself not to harm or pillage the Temple. In their fury, the soldiers went out of control, spurred on by the Zealots who had vowed to fight to the death and were fighting them every inch of the way, from column to column, along the balustrades, and from room to room. The soldiers went berserk in the slaughter—and they began pulling down the Temple itself. They did not stop until it lay in rubble. Because, outside the Temple, on the orders of Vespasian, the Roman army was systematically using its machines of war against the city itself and did not leave a single edifice standing. How long it took to make rubble of Jerusalem I do not know, but they removed the rubble in carts drawn by oxen and then they harrowed the ground, leveling it as flat as possible. In the center of this wasteland they raised a single stele and they inscribed in three languages the warning that here was once the site of Jerusalem and this is what happens to cities that defy Rome.

This happened in the year 70 of the Common Era. Palestine lost its protectorate status and came directly under the rule of Rome.

We do not know how many generations, but there must have been at least one generation of surviving Jews who hid in caves and in the mountains and in the desolate places of the land of Israel the Romans called "Palestine." What they thought and felt as they passed what was once Jerusalem I doubt words could describe. Only around Tiberius, in the Galilee, were the Jews granted a degree of self-government. This was where the Jewish schools flourished for a while. But the resistance of the

Jews continued, and within two generations after the destruction of the Temple the resistance grew into open revolts and called up a leader by the name of Bar Kochba. Bar Kochba was not his real name but the name given to him by those he inspired. It means "son of the star." Bar Kochba struck the first mint of coins since Jerusalem was destroyed, and organized the revolutionaries in a war of liberation. Akiva likened Bar Kochba to the messiah. (Rabbi Akiva was martyred, flayed alive while he laughed in the faces of the Roman soldiers and recited the Sh'ma firmly in a loud voice as he died—an example followed later by the Sephardim of Spain when they were burned at the stake during the Inquisition.) Bar Kochba was a brilliant strategist and organizer and fought the Romans for three years. He was eventually defeated at Betar. This time, in putting down the resistance, the Romans were killing every Jew in Palestine and they made the whole land desolate. The Jews were forced irrevocably to go into exile or to live as fugitives in their own land, a land once considered so holy a king in Babylon had boxes of the soil spread on the dais so that his throne rested in it. After Rome completely defeated and crushed the revolution, killing Bar Kochba at Betar, they destroyed the land and made it barren and burned down the houses in the countryside. This was the end of a long period of resistance against foreign domination which some date as beginning around the time of Herod's death. Bar Kochba was defeated in the year 135. The revolts he caused lasted for three years and historians say it was "suppressed by Romans with widespread destruction." The Jews had been dispersed in all the lands within the Roman Empire, which by then included all of Europe "this side of the Rhine." The Jews maintained their communal existence and held fast to Judaism, following the exile tradition first begun by the visionary prophet Ezekiel. The Jews, with their little families, brought enlightenment and human values to the savage peoples of Europe who were crushed by the barbarism that was Rome.

Although the population of the Jews in their homeland was decimated and strangers from other lands constituted the majority, the Jews still populated their lands. Prejudice and discrimination against the Jews was always greater in their homelands than in the nations they dispersed to. The peoples and their generations who came and went from the Jewish homeland (for over eighteen hundred years) had contempt for the Jews—the natives—and the rise of Jewish power and self-determination.

Five years after Bar Kochba was killed, the Emperor at Rome (Hadrian), to obliterate the memory of Jerusalem, rebuilt it as a Roman provincial city and he named it *Aelia Capitolina*. The Jewish lands were now considered "romanized." But Rome itself was in its death throes, and when Constantine I, a Christian, came to the throne in the city now named Istanbul, his mother Helena converted Aelia Capitolina into a Christian city and restored its name to Jerusalem. This occurred in 313. The center of power had shifted from Rome to what is now Istanbul and from the fourth to the sixth century the Jewish homeland was ruled by the Eastern Byzantine Empire.

When the Byzantine Emperor made it a Christian city and restored the name "Jerusalem" it must have been a period in which the Jews in the land of Israel became recipients of Christian charity—so long as they remembered the *via dolorosa*. In their own way, the Jews may have begun to lead a semblance of a normal life. They were blamed by the vast multitude of strangers in their land for the destruction of Jerusalem and the House of G-d. Every minute of every day, among these strangers who had taken their homeland for their showplace, the Jews were punished and admonished for the death of god. This peculiar kind of persecution has probably never appeared on this earth before. Loving Christian arms reached out to embrace them and to lift them up out of poverty and despair and drew them to a Christian bosom fraught with snares, devices of torture, defamation, and a hatred so perverse as to call up in the memory the tales of the demons that once lived in the gutters and alleys of old Babylon. Love and hate revolved inevitably, each in turn, through every transaction with the Christian strangers in their land.

For a short period during the first part of the seventh century, Persians took Palestine as a prize of war until about 636 C.E. Then the Arab Moslems snatched it in the name of Islam.

We do not know exactly when the custom began, but the Jews outside the land of Israel sent relief in the form of a few alms to support the scholars and the holy men among the Jews living in hovels in Jerusalem who kept watch and prayed for the messiah. I think this began shortly after the Islamic religion sprang into existence on the edge of a sword that swept the known world, seizing Jerusalem as one of its first prizes. The Moslems erected a mosque over the site of the House of G-d and sought out the holy places and the inheritance of Israel in order to add to their booty the jewels of Israel. O how the people must have wept when they looked at Jerusalem! There was no Christian charity in the land. A Jew could not dispute and defend his goods (or his life) in a Moslem court of law. The Jews were required by the Koran to dress in a certain manner so they could be recognized at a glance. The laws that were codified out of the Koran subordinated the Jews to these strangers in their land in almost every detail of private and personal life. How they walked along a street, how they bowed to a Moslem, how they spoke to a Moslem, how they surrendered their property to a Moslem—all of this and more was worked out in fine detail—and the Jews in the land of Israel walked under this burden for centuries. All the resentment and prejudice that the Christians conceal—all the latent hatred—all the things in the bosom of Christianity's outstretched loving arms were now out in the open and no longer a secret snare waiting for every Jew behind the smiling friendship of every Christian. It was because of this that Jews might look back on the Moslem captivity of the land of Israel as a more just captivity. They knew their place with the Moslems and there were no pretenses involving pity.

The persecution of the Jews was turned into a religion codified in the Koran. The Koran records litany after litany of injunctions against the Jews and long harangues against Israel. The Prophet of the Moslems took up the burden of Hagar and Ishmael against Isaac and Jacob, claiming that all the possessions and inheritance of Israel rightfully belonged to Ishmael and his descendants, the Moslems. The Moslems could not conceal their hatred.

The Jewish homeland next passed again into the hands of Istanbul— no longer Byzantine but now Islamic Turkey—around 1070. Then, about thirty years later, the Christian Crusades came in the name of freeing Jerusalem from Islam. In 1250 the Mamelukes of Egypt took Jerusalem as a prize and held it for almost three hundred years, until it once more fell by war in 1517 to the Ottoman Turks. It became a provincial backwater of the Turkish Empire until the twentieth century, when it became a protectorate of Britain.

Throughout eighteen centuries of foreign domination of one power after another, what the Greeks called the "Palestine" was always inhabited by the original natives, the Jews. The Palestine sat at the geographical hub of world commerce, and it was for this reason that all the various nationalities passed to and fro in the land as it went under the rule of at least ten great foreign nations. The peoples who occupied the Jewish homeland did not once fight for the liberation of the Palestine from foreign domination. The Jews could not fight for the liberation of their land, not only because they were a minority, but also because the majority population *always* collaborated with the foreign power. The Palestine had a majority population of compradors. They were part of peoples that generally became known as Levantines and they were mostly centered in the Lebanon and along the southern coast of Turkey.

Just before the turn of the century, the Jews in the Palestine began their struggle with Turkey and the Levantine inhabitants for political self-determination in their own country. By the time Great Britain took possession of it the Jews in the Palestine had begun again, as in the days of Bar Kochba, to fight openly for the liberation of the country. The Levantine population followed the Islamic way of life and the Imams (the Moslem fundamentalist religious leaders) preached against the Jews. In searching for a political solution to their problems, the Jews divided over whether they should as a man drive the British out and ignore the Levantines or try to make an alliance with them against Britain as a common enemy—and then settle their differences after they had liberated the country. Those who believed they could form an alliance with the non-Jewish population, and together drive out the British, were sadly mistaken and were led by betrayal into the gallows and garrisons of the British. Everyone collaborated with the British occupation against the Jews, as one Jewish resistance fighter after another was imprisoned or executed by the British colonial government. Jews throughout Russia and east Central Europe were being driven out by national liberation movements—and some of them went home to help liberate their homeland. The Jews, as the nationalist movements spread over western Europe, began to come home. When Nazi Germany and its allied movements devastated western civilization itself, it was at the cost of over six million Jews. The struggle for independence intensified in the Palestine. After a war of resistance that lasted from the 1880s to 1947, a small parcel of territory was finally liberated and the British mandate was withdrawn at the United Nations. The Moslem, non-Jewish inhabitants petitioned first Great Britain itself and then the United Nations to keep the Palestine under foreign British occupation. They were compradors to the very end. The day the liberation of Jewish territory was completed and the state of Israel was finally under a Jewish government, the non-Jewish population began attacking Jews and, using what influence they had, invited other surrounding Moslem nations to invade Israel. They called themselves "Palestinians," a designation that did not come into existence until Israel had become a state. The people who today call themselves "Palestinians" yesterday called themselves by the names of a wide range of Semitic ethnic groups and by the names of various Moslem religious sects. They were usually thought of as Lebanese or simply "Arabs." They had never cared for the land or the upkeep of the little towns and villages, and most of Jerusalem was a slum city. The liberation of the Jewish homeland entailed the return of the foreign populations to their various homelands for that reason. Most of the population employed itself in merchandise trade and ranged nomadically all along the trade centers of the Middle East. They had no population of farmers except (at the most) traditional self-sufficient communities—so fragile and backward that the introduction of something as common as a tractor would have upset the whole balance and dispersed the community. They *knew* that the land they occupied was Jewish. They always knew it was not their land, and instead of honoring the Jews and respecting their rights, they spat on them and in the name of the Koran imposed what amounted to prison restrictions on the Jews.

The government of Israel, in order to defend the Jews, ordered the offending non-Jewish population to disperse and asked the surrounding Moslem nations to gather in their people. In violation of their own Koran, they refused to take them in.

In the Arab nation of Jordan the Jordanian army surrounded large "Palestinian" settlements inside the borders of Jordan and used tanks and fire bombs against their fellow Moslems. The "Palestinians" responded to this by blaming Israel and forming terrorist groups financed by Moslem governments. The most famous one called itself Black September. That black September was the month their settlements were attacked, not by Jews or Israel, but by Arab Jordanian soldiers. Instead of attacking Jordan in response, they sought help from Jordan's Arab allies and set up "Palestinian liberation organizations" in Egypt, Libya, Algeria, Lebanon, Syria (and, yes, in Jordan itself) and declared war on Israel. The compradors had become mercenaries. The existence of Israel upset the balance of power of the feudal ruling classes and families of the Arab nations, and they use the "Palestinians" as a way to constantly question the legitimacy of the state of Israel—which has the mandate not only of all the Jews in the Mid-East but in the western world as well. The Moslems have a religion openly directed against Israel and the Jews. This is not just an interpretation of the Koran; the Koran bluntly states these doctrines. The "Palestinians" are not socialists or Marxists or communists or even democrats. They are *Moslems.*

The Moslem way of life is directed against the Jews and Israel as the possessor of all that belongs to them. The Koran is a book of laws which governs their entire culture. Moslems, for example, cannot live in western Europe because of the democratic rights women and children possess and because of the property laws. The legal relations that exist within and between families in western civilization contradict Moslem laws that govern relations within and between families. We understand this in western civilizations. This was why, after the Moors were defeated in early European history, the Moslems in hordes evacuated Europe and went back to Moslem lands.

Although we understand this, we seem to find it difficult to understand that, even if not for the same reasons, the Moslems cannot coexist with Israelis. If it were a matter of social democratic contact between the Israelis and the Moslems it would be simple. But the world is not an abstraction and it is not possible for the Moslems to live in Israel without disliking the Jews, because that is their religion—their custom, tradition, their way of life. What the "Palestinians" want is to use the democratic slogans we understand in the west to make it appear that Israel is in violation of a democracy they themselves have never practiced. If they did practice it, they would have had to commit the Koran to the flames.

This is most clear in the animosity of Moslem nations toward Israel. Israel is fighting a war for the liberation of its territories and for self-determination among the nations.

As always,
Jack

Dear B. Alpert,

What I think is most significant about the *luftmensch* is his *existent* relation to his society—a society which is not *luftmensch;* a society which makes him *luftmensch.*

The general definition of a *luftmensch* is one of mixed race, with the peculiarity that in appearance he is taken to be of only one race. This is the race of the society he lives in, united (as a society) by bonds of common affection and custom. It is really no more (in concept) than a very large family.

We can take for example any two races, but I will take the Asiatic and the European as an example.

It must be understood here that the *luftmensch* was reared from childhood to identify himself with one or the other race. Let us say he is reared as a Chinese, in Chinese society. Let us say this Chinese society is in close proximity to a European society and that one of his parents was English, and the other Chinese. His external appearance is Chinese. In fact, let us say he develops into a cultivated man in the Chinese society. He knows more about Chinese culture than does the average Chinese man.

But that would be to make exception, so let us say he is merely an ordinary common man (which would not be possible).

For some reason (let us say his hair is soft and wavy) any Chinese who scrutinizes him for any reason can detect a "drop" of European blood. He would suffer a loss of affection from the people his affections are tied up in (the Chinese people)—not a loss of love on *his* part, but on the part of his society at large (Chinese).

In his entire lifetime, seldom would any acquaintance ever mention it *explicitly*. But reference would be made to it in colloquial allusions he would never understand. He would simply think his experience of life is the experience of life of everyone around him, that people are naturally cold and full of disappointment. He would think it "Chinese." The humanity of a people is determined by the quality of its love and the depth of its tolerance.

Let us say there were times he wore his hair cut so short no one could detect that it was wavy and therefore could not detect that "drop" of European blood: He would be privy to the secret prejudices of the common Chinese toward Europeans. He would live in fear that someone would detect his European blood. He would hate himself.

His life could be said to have been ruined. He would *be* a tragedy.

If he educated himself, it would place him between two worlds (the Chinese and the European) *consciously*.

If the European and the Chinese, as two distinct and major racial groups, are destined to meld into one, then this *luftmensch* occupies a temporal position: He *is* the future. He knows the best and the worst of both worlds. He would have no *choice*. Let me quickly add that it is not possible that the European and the Chinese could vanish as distinct races. What I mean to say is that (in theory) in the interactions between them a new social mass arises: A *majority* population of "Eurasians." The Chinese and the European would persist as distinct and separate societies, but they would no longer be the masters and dominate the *luftmensch*. How would he look at them? With affection, the affection one has for quaint, charming antiques. With amusement. Even, finally, with love.

—This is what in fact happened to the blood-Greek, the blood-Roman, the blood-Aryan (of India of the ancient world, of course). We all love them.

The interesting thing (as I said) is the *temporal* position the *luftmensch* occupies. It is a tremendous advantage but a dangerous position so far as his personal well-being is concerned (his internal development). His usual fate is prison or the madhouse. For him the same concept (or feeling) can have two conflicting meanings—one Chinese and the other English.

The ancient Law of Manu subsumed this semantic problem but erred in turning habit ("custom") into *caste*. This problem arises with the withering away of the nation-state historically. We are beginning to be faced with it now. It is a problem of specie-being.

Best wishes,
Jack

Dear Bob,

I was perhaps not clear with you because of the vagueness of what is meant when someone accuses someone else of being a "literalist" in understanding the meaning of the bible. I am not a literalist but it is not clear that I am not a literalist because those who have popularized this term have never properly defined it. It is used somewhat the way the term "philistine" is used in name-calling.

The only examples of "literalism" I have seen appear in anti-religious criticisms of the bible and in anti-Judaic attempts to abscond with it and draw it into another religious sphere outside Judaism. The main examples of the fallacy of applying a literal interpretation to the bible are found in applying the standards of scientific empiricism to it. (Scientific *standards* and scientific empiricism are not the same thing.) For instance, not long ago it was refuted scientifically on the grounds that certain ancient cities (for example, Ur) did not exist and that it was medically impossible for anyone to live as long as certain persons in the bible lived. These kind of arguments assume the same things *in the reading* of the bible as the religious fundamentalists assume, but for opposite purposes. What is striking (and not a little amusing) is that the scientists who refute the bible are addressing themselves to semi-literate clodhoppers who do not understand a word they are saying. These are their only opponents. They might as well write scientific dissertations proving that there is no Santa Clause, despite what children think.

The factual knowledge that learned men had in early antiquity (Egypt and Babylonia, for example), was presupposed in the composition of at least the first five books of the bible (the Torah). These presuppositions were scientific in nature, in a deeper sense than empiricism is scientific today (the merely empirical fact). It was that but encompassed much more. Science began with knowledge of the human being *and then* encompassed knowledge of the natural universe. We probably do not have today even a fraction of the knowledge of the human being that was known in earliest antiquity.

But there are more pressing examples of literalism and these are political. These are dangerous accusations leveled by fundamentalists and political scientists alike. The most pressing example is the example of Israel. On the one hand, the fundamentalists (Moslem as well as Christian) argue that according to their respective religions the land of Israel does not belong to Jews, even though they recognize it is their homeland. It turns out to be one of the *leitmotifs* of both these religions and is based on mystical revelations outside the bible.

The political scientists, on the other hand, charge that the bible, where it outlines the territorial boundaries of the land of Israel, only outlines a "spiritual nation." They charge that any claim to the land that can be supported by the Torah is a *fundamentalist* claim—and in this manner they brand men like Rabbi Kahane as fundamentalists no different from Christian or Moslem fundamentalists, simply because the Rabbi demands the return of all of Israel without compromise. The political scientists wrongly accuse him of the fallacy of "literalism."

There is no point in going into the various theories of either the fundamentalists or the empirical scientists in their explanations of the bible. For a great many sound reasons I am convinced the Torah was not a product of the human mind.

But the assaults on the Torah *are* a product of the human mind and seem to run parallel to assaults on the Jewish people historically. The objective history of Jews throughout the world is almost exclusively the history of a people who have renounced violence and have of necessity had to defend themselves with non-violent means.

Up until around the seventeenth century the Jewish ghettos defended themselves with the religious consolation of resting safely in Zion, like a man resting in a tiny boat as it is tossed on the waves of the sea raging around him. This was how they practiced the love of their destiny *(amor fati)*.

There were Jews who thought Napoleon was the messiah when he liberated some of the ghettos of Europe. The same was said of Bismark for the same reasons. They were quicky disillusioned, however. It was around the seventeenth century that politics and political parties began to come into existence.

Before then people were *subjects* and not *citizens*. After the ghettos were liberated, Jews and other minorities, along with the majority, enjoyed a higher status than that of mere subject. They became citizens, one and all. Naturally, Jews took part in various political parties with their non-Jewish counterparts. But during crises, Jews (along with other ethnic minorities) took the brunt of the hardships and, progressively, took the *blame* for the crises themselves. Jews could no longer defend themselves as they had traditionally in the ghettos. The other ethnic minorities had their own countries they could return to. They shared in their persons the degree of formidability their particular countries had in relation to other countries. In other words, if the Italians in Austria were being persecuted as Italians, Italy could stop it even if it meant war. But Jews did not have this line of defense, which has proved to be absolutely essential, especially since the Holocaust.

Religious Zionism, the belief that the messiah would appear and lead them peacefully back to the land of Israel, gave way to a more practical conception of Zionism. This occurred through non-violent methods of self-defense which accumulated and evolved with anti-Semitic attacks, after Jews were emancipated from the ghettos. The Jews gradually took their destiny into their own hands, just as every other nation does. It is called "Zionism" and it is not a political ideology for the simple reason that it is only a self-defense mechanism. In the bare bones of the matter, national liberation is not itself an ideology or even an "idea"—no more than the phenomena of self-preservation can be called an "ideology."

Israel's demand for the liberation of its territories is not an ideology but a territorial claim no one can in reality deny—including the fundamentalists and political scientists. The grounds of *their* possible denials are ideological.

This is clear in the ideology of the Arab nations today, as ever.

When the United Nations voted in favor of giving some of the territory back to Israel and ending the British mandate, the Arab nations as a solid bloc voted in opposition. They voted knowing that it was the homeland of the Jews and with the specific purpose of disenfranchising the Jews because of racial hatred of Jews. The United Nations is a democratic assembly, which means that, although some nations might disagree with the majority decision, they must not obstruct it on penalty of violating the rule of democracy and being expelled from the United Nations.

The Moslem Koran, which is the very foundation of the Arab nations, blatantly denounces Jewish people in racist terms unequalled anywhere. It boldly and viciously wills openly the destruction of the land of Israel. The Koran is a document unique among all religions of the world for its endless preaching of hate and racism.

And yet the Arab nations have succeeded in getting a resolution passed in the United Nations equating Zionism with racism. How was this possible?

Most of us misjudge the competence of the Arab nations. We fail to realize that their cultures and their cities rest upon the rubble of the ancient world. Peoples of the Arab nations can trace their line directly into the ancient world. They are much older and wiser in the ways of human beings. They are as our elder brothers. We are naive children to them. All they need do is smile and be kind to us and manipulate our sense of justice and pity. It is in the Arab world that they see us coming and pretend to be blind or deaf and dumb or feeble-minded or crippled or diseased—as they beg for pity in their costumes of rags. They never enact these charades before their own people. They are different from us not because of their race but because of their ancient culture which has inhibited their economic development. An ancient order hangs over them like the sword of Damocles. There is a class which includes *millions* in the Arab world who are educated in the West and are well-to-do economically. They claim to be enlightened and they know that every word I have written here is true. None of them would have the gall to *deny* it but all of them pretend to regret the condition of "their people" and to deny their racial prejudice against Jews (and others) dictated by the Koran. These college graduates of the West do not talk about transforming the Arab nations politically and economically into modern democracies. They talk about Israel's mistreatment of Arab "freedom fighters," whom the Arab nations recruit against Israel and in violation of the United Nations.

The "Palestinians" constitute an army of irregulars in a united Arab war against Israel and the government of the United Nations. This is why nations that finance and foster in their territories "Palestinian freedom fighters" are in violation of the democratic rule of the United Nations.

I hope this answers your question and clears up your misconceptions.

Sincerely,
Jack

Dear Mashey,

Everyone understands that consciousness is only the tip of an iceberg and has roots deep in the organism. It is very difficult (if not impossible) to *consciously* tap the roots of consciousness. The whole spectrum of inherited disposition constitutes this from which consciousness arises (Neumann's *Origin of Consciousness* explains this, but laboratory experiments support it as well). Intellectual intuition draws a great deal on this area. It has been referred to as a kind of memory as well.

I do not know if Albert Einstein (to name but one among many great men in science, especially since the nineteenth century) ever read the ancient texts or was otherwise versed in oral traditions, but when I read the *Bereshith* I was struck by the mentality of the Companions in their sage discussion of the origin of the universe and by the *mentality* of Einstein's marvelous mind.

Whether it is true or not, I cannot be persuaded that this played no major role in Einstein's peculiar (and gigantic) genius in physics.

Everything in *Bereshith* is Einsteinian—the "shapeless center enclosed in a ring"; the "supernal point"; the "Central Column"; the "turning in Left and Right"; the "grades"; the "sparks" (and so on; this is only a small sampling of the conceptions employed). All of this can relate to electromagnetic flux, and even the "three vowel points, combined with each other to form one entity" resembles the notion of the addition of the dimension of time to the three dimensions of space to form "unified fields" ("one entity")—all of it suggests the Einsteinian mentality. I could almost envision the creation of gravitating masses.

None of the sages were what we call "philosophers"—but they were *scientific* in a sense much greater than the Greeks (including the school of Aristotle). A Hebrew word was a *datum,* a *fact;* not an abstraction.

But (for our purposes here) that too is beside the point. Western philosophy developed out of Medieval metaphysics (religious metaphysics of the "Medieval Philosophers"). All the philosophical concepts and subjects of the West were metaphysical originally. It is my notion that the mentality of the oral traditions of the teaching will reach its secular development not in a debunking but in a *scientific* comprehension of man, the earth—in short, the universe. In a sense, Spinoza was the Kant of this tradition and he stands in the same relation to science (as properly conceived) as Kant stands to German philosophy. The misfortunes of Spinoza's life (expulsion, excommunication) were caused by the absence of religious emancipation in Europe (on both sides of the "fence") and fanatical attacks on free thought (again, on both sides of the "fence").

I think it was with Spinoza that a certain kind of "geometrical reasoning" began that resulted in religious emancipation in Europe; with Spinoza the principle of dialectic was first stated, which found its way into the mind of Kant and culminated in Hegelian philosophy (*determino est nego*). This principle was first demonstrated in Spinoza's *Ethica* that man masters his passions by the act of determining them. They are determined by their ultimate value—not their *immediate* value (animals have the immediate form of consciousness).

Spinoza's *Ethica* is not a *metaphysical* system. All of the emotions Spinoza dealt with in the *Ethica* are emotions all animals also feel. They all feel anger, love, hate, joy, curiosity, fear, awe, wonder, greed, lust, embarrassment, and so on.

The ancient Judeans had no ontology, no metaphysics. The question of whether or not God exists was as meaningless to them as the question of whether or not they themselves existed: It was a nonsense question. The way letters were combined to construct words and the way words were combined to construct sentences made it impossible to raise ontological questions.

The only questions that could be raised were the meaning and application of the Torah. In this sense, Spinoza was more Judean than any Jewish secular thinker. Properly speaking, what we ordinarily think of as "metaphysics" (in the cabbala literature) is not metaphysics at all. The Torah was applied scientifically. This is what distinguishes cabbala from metaphysics. It is a scientific attitude par excellence to be unable to comprehend a question pertaining to the *nature* of God or to be unable to discuss the question of whether or not God exists.

One could say metaphysics is a product of putting the intelligence under the command of the passions and that science is a product of putting the emotions under the command of the intelligence.

It could be possible that we have in Spinoza's *Ethica* the theoretical means of solving the problem of emotional contagions of irrationality by the use of "geometrical reasoning." If so, then an emotional problem that grips the masses can be solved by guiding the emotions geometrically.

Do practical means of communication of ideas exist (in sufficiency) to accomplish this? If so, then every contagious emotional problem could be treated successfully as a problem in geometry, in which each determination is posited as a predicate. By the reasoning inherent in the method, the ideas Spinoza referred to as self-generating would be a development of presuppositions in the psyche. Every emotion in the *Ethica* would lead to an equation.

The means by which Spinoza set himself free as a moral person could be the means by which a moral nation sets itself free among other nations.

The manner in which the word "sophist" has come to be used in the expression "sophistication" does not really do justice to the ancient philosophers who founded the Sophist school. I say this because I believe that the acquisition of knowledge should be honored above all else, even when a system of education is only put into effect for the sole purpose of making a person merely *appear* to be educated. This appearance of course has no substance in learning. Its real substance is drawn from the same waters as politeness and civilized social behavior. Mere sophistication serves the purpose of at least placing a high social value on learning, which, relatively speaking, not everyone is capable of.

It is in this sense that I would have agreed with the old gaonate. Among real scholars no one worries about sophistication or being "duped" by anyone's chatter. I think a real scholar is on the contrary charmed by such ornamental people.

I do not think Spinoza could have written the *Ethica* if he were not persecuted. He was able to grasp the reality of the body and enlighten others to the fallacies of Descartes's scientific theories because of this.

Someone said thinking is really more closely related to dancing than to the strict forms of logic, and I think that must have been the deeper purpose behind the *musar* idea originally. Rhythm (music) is of course at the essence of all dancing. It is not difficult to acknowledge, at least in some categories, that truth is painful. In fact, in some areas the test of a truth might very well be whether or not it causes pain to the knower.

Physiological responses to truth would of course be manifest in tears—but of course there would be a great many more subtle organic manifestations in the body. We know cognition is affected and, subsequently, its companion perceptions.

The thoughts (if I may be permitted to speak in this manner) would in this case be undeniably related to dancing. And this implies the music (the rhythms), which may be less manifest but must surely be the product of internal physiological movements of some kind.

Pain and pleasure, as we all know, are merely two sides of the same coin. This is why the prophets who experienced the chastisement of G-d rejoiced in their afflictions.

I think this is the power of persecution: that one *knows* each of us is alone, and no society, no matter how outwardly united or just or *humane*—no matter how good a society is—it is never of greater value than the value of its individuals.

All societies have ways of defending themselves, if not against each other then against the destructive elements of their environment. And all societies have defended themselves against other societies. Societies have self-defense systems (one might say). To one degree or another, with a few exceptions due to isolation, every society has a warrior tradition.

Societies that are dominated by their warrior traditions seldom (if ever) have produced a *sage*. The individual in such societies, if he is shunned by his society and persecuted, usually, if he survives, becomes masterful in martial self-defense. You see, even this knowledge, wrought in the fires of persecution, is knowledge of the *body*. Thought, in other words, returns to its abode and fortifies its house.

Self-defense (self-preservation) has its real examples only in individuals and not societies.

Someone who has erred fundamentally and suffers from society, even though society does not actively persecute him, has strayed from himself without knowing it. What he learns if he survives is not Socratic knowledge of self but of others. He thinks, for example, that others are something they are not, because he mistakes the feelings of others for his own feelings. The pain brings him to knowledge of what *causes* pain in general and not to knowledge of his "unique self."

Without this experience I do not think the learning of ethics can be anything but sophistication—"Sophist knowledge." The ethics of the fathers, it seems to me, realizes this whereas no other recorded discussion has ever done so. It understood ethical categories outside the realm of ethical behavior in its comprehension of the relation between the self and others. It understood the *ethos* of unethical thinking. On the basis of one's timely ethical experience of life, the higher law has greater meaning and application. All else is dogma.

The rejection of this truth, of course, can and does lead to sophism. But a *system* of education based on persecution is a higher discipline than can be found anywhere in the world today or in the past. The most severe yoga discipline is childish nonsense beside this. This is a scientific system of learning and it is rooted in mankind—and not in some abstract theorem of the universe, as Aristotle and the sophists would have it. Which, I think, was at the bottom of the complaints of the original *musars*. It will always be true that the order of human society will be rooted in laws that reflect the continuity of the phenomena of nature and the individual. The laws of such an order can never be ratified by a democratic assembly.

Sincerely,
Jack

Dear Norman,

The Nazi theory of culture can almost exclusively be traced to theories of the state in ancient Greece and to Richard Wagner's theories, which postulated that *volk* culture originated in legends and customs the *volk* passed on to each other in oral traditions from observing the adventures of their aristocratic rulers. The Nazi theory postulated that only those of noble birth could suffer greatly and therefore be tragic figures. The Nazi theory postulated that those holding great possessions and great positions of power in the world suffered tragically when those possessions were lost or when they fell from power. The Nazi theory postulated that tragedy begins in a reach for more power in this world but only by the masters who possess *all* the power in the world. The Nazis acquired this outlook from Richard Wagner and a few scholarly mistakes of cognition Nietzsche made in *The Birth of Tragedy,* a work in which Nietzsche did not understand his youthful self—as he so eloquently confessed in *Ecce Homo,* where he said things like: ". . . Wherever you see the name Wagner in those early writings you should put my name or the name Zarathustra." Or where he wrote: "I did not understand the spirit I carried in me." Et cetera.

No one argues against the idea that tragedy had its earliest beginnings in music. I am going to distinguish between tragedy as a staged production (with a script, actors, costumes, etc.) and tragedy as nothing but music. This tragedy as nothing but music is something I will call by the name of *tragoidia*—since it is the etymological root of the origin of our English word "tragedy." Dancing would be to the *tragoidia* what acting is to tragedy. It originated in ancient Greece and means "song of the he-goat." A he-goat, since it bears no offspring and gives no milk, was of less value than a she-goat. I do not think that tragedy has exalted origins. It had humble origins, just as the blues, just as *fado* music, just as the music Piaf made for the French (and her counterparts of Spain and Mexico today). Just as this was and is "humble music," so too was the *tragoidia.* It had to have been the music of those who had no status and no property—the music of those who had nothing. Their losses, then, could not be estimated. Only such people originally figured in the *tragoidia.*

Tragedy then came into existence as an art form in classic Greece (after the archaic period) when suffering was first appropriated from the *tragoidia* and the protagonist was crowned king and set upon a stage. That was the death of *tragoidia.* Tragedy became a means of appropriating the suffering of those who were sung about in the *tragoidia.* There is evidence in sources from archaic Greece that the *tragoidia* had a subversive effect on slaves and the dispossessed people of the land. Poets of *tragoidia* roamed the lands of the earliest Greek rulers singing for a pittance and bringing news from abroad. This was probably why Plato, in a later age, advised that in his well-governed *Republic* these poets should be outlawed, banished.

The *tragoidia* was not originally a choral ensemble of lyres, flutes, cymbals, and ivory-encased drums, played to elegantly reclining Athenians. It was the voice of that suffering many-stringed instrument, man. It was sung by those set adrift in a chaotic world, where the dice were always loaded against them. They thought it was "fate" but the masters of Greece knew better. Oedipus, before he was crowned and translated from the *tragoidia* to tragedy, was probably a slave without rights, property, and of less value or status in ancient Greece than a he-goat. He was probably born into slavery and did not know who his mother and his father were. His story would pivot on a common fact of slave-life, but with a few twists: By some fluke he would learn that his wife (probably given to him for a mate) was his mother and his father was someone he had killed accidentally in a youthful brawl with another slave. The citizens of Greece, when they heard this song, probably could not comprehend how a slave could suffer and despair at this knowledge. Slaves were not genuine human beings to them.

This is why in the origins of tragedy a criminal was never a tragic figure. The figures of the *tragoidia* did not recognize the category of criminal. Although this is probably a more questionable discussion both of Oedipus and the origins of tragedy than has ever been presented, and one that turns the classic theory upside down, anyone would be hard put to argue otherwise about the origins of tragedy in the *tragoidia*. There are *tragoidia* singers today in the Latin world (Italy, Portugal, Mexico) who have maintained the tradition of making it a form of weeping—and I think that is what it originally was. It served the same fundamental purpose weeping serves universally. It creates empathy. Aristotle, descended from the Socratic school, misunderstood this in his theory of *catharsis*. Empathy is not pity.

The main emotion the *tragoidia* would evoke (in the midst of its frightening and dreadful aspect) would have been the emotion of envy and admiration for the figures of the *tragoidia*. Not *pity*. This envy, this *desire* for the terrible (and the terrible wisdom it would impart), was perhaps the leading motive in appropriating it. The envy of any suffering which confers greatness is probably as ancient as sexual jealousy in human beings, particularly among those who have power and status in the world.

My theory, that tragedy was appropriated by the citizens of Greece from the *tragoidia,* is just as significant aesthetically as the transition from an auditory art form of rhythms to a visual art form of images. For example, the music of Richard Wagner is nothing but tone-painting. He begins with the image and enshrines it in music. In doing so he destroys the universality of music. His was a transition to operatic forms which have no meaning outside of a specific time and place.

But the original appropriation was the *appropriation of suffering* by those who wanted to acquire the experience of others. This mechanism is known, and a few decades ago the intellectuals made it a fashionable subject in analyses of how the suffering of black Americans (expressed in their music) was appropriated by their former masters.

I think this is a source of cruelty. According to thinkers both in late antiquity and today, the movements of tragedy on a stage developed, brought to fruition, and harvested before the eyes what was terrifying in human existence. The audience of the tragedy, suspended in mounting terror, saw the terror dramatically confronted in time and space on the stage—with great admiration. But what is most terrifying in human existence is perhaps not something that enters through the sense of touch and vision. Perhaps it enters through the sense of hearing and speech. There were curses among the Mycenaeans of ancient Crete so terrible they could not be visualized (only chanted); terrors no scene in dimensional time and space could imprison. I think when the *tragoidia* became tragedy it had an *anesthetic* effect on sensitivity to pain, affecting the central nervous system like an illusion. It imparted a delusion of profound experience and it instilled illusory feelings of being *masterful,* "heroic." The *pathos* of distance here opened an infinite abyss aesthetically. This is how cruelty, as I have noted, came into existence: by *watching* the suffering of others from outside. The ancient Greeks were the most pitiless people in antiquity. The knowledge of how to torment the human being was sought after in classic Greece and is still sought after today in the tragedy. And here, in this sphere of contemplation, we have departed not only from the *tragoidia* (and tragic wisdom, rooted in intuitions of eternal recurrence), but from the entire subject of tragedy itself. It was in this sphere of contemplation Aristotle meditated erroneously on tragedy. It explains why the examination of the suffering of the tragic figure became focused on the *character.* Tragedy then became the result of a flaw in character deriving from a metaphysical disharmony between the character of the tragic figure and existence. This mode of contemplation took tragedy *beyond* reality and into a mental realm of good and evil, which was later incorporated into the *foundation* of Christian theology and theological speculation. I would say that this was how it was possible for Christianity to weep before the sufferings of a writhing god nailed to a cross and at the same time feel scorn and contempt toward the sufferings of mortals around them. In the name of a god of love it was in this way possible for his worshippers to practice without sin the very opposite. Suffering was taken beyond reality. We enter the metaphysical sphere. This is what, in less extravagant terms, Nietzsche meant when he condemned Socratic wisdom and took up the ancient cant against Socrates as one possessed daemonically. He blamed Socrates for destroying the tragedy. Therefore, in the tragedy classic to western Europe (which is modeled on the Greek), it is safe to understand the tragic figure as one possessed—as someone with status and power haunted by metaphysical forces and mad compulsions in conflicts over power.

Those with power have always been removed and immune from the wisdom suffering imparts. When it comes, it is a catastrophe so bizarre it is incomprehensible. It strikes *daemonically,* from outside, and drags the so-called "tragic figure" down the stairs of power into the world of common men—which to him is an abyss of madness. This was the "tragedy" of Nebuchadnezzar which literally brought him down on all fours, grazing like a beast in the fields.

The appropriation of the suffering of the Jews is so universal and so ancient that I would say this is where the cruelty I have spoken of had its *most general* beginnings. It is most aptly described in a very ancient song which tells how the Jews, taken into slavery in Babylon, were forced to sing their sacred songs of worship for the entertainment of the Babylonians. It tells how they were forced to sing and be merry for the Babylonians, even as they sat in chains and wept: "By the waters of Babylon, there we sat down, yea, we wept when we remembered. . ." The House of G-d was in ruin and they were slaves now in a foreign land. This song goes on to describe how they strung their harps upon the willows by the river, because the Babylonians were forcing them to sing and make merry with perhaps one of the most sacred and solemn canticles of their worship in the desolated Temple at Jerusalem. They shouted the command at the Jews sitting and weeping beofre them: "Sing us one of your songs of Zion!" The song which tells this story is a song whose refrain goes something like this: *"How long must we sing the Lord's song in a strange land?"*

Ever since these events happened as described in this song, the appropriation of the suffering of the Jews has occurred everywhere they or their holy scriptures (the Torah) appeared. Two of the most general appropriations, but by no means the only ones, were the Islamic and the Christian religions. But the one thing that could never be appropriated was the *wisdom* gained from their experience. The understanding which appropriated the suffering of the Jews would have, therefore, in the light of what I have noted about cruelty, had to have been a daemonic understanding, an understanding outside reality and imprisoned in lies. This implies that those who appropriate the sufferings of others are doomed to daemonic destruction—just as the *tragoidia* was appropriated by classic Greek tragedy, the classic Greek tragic figure was doomed to become a man possessed by an acquisition appropriated at the cost of his soul.

Enough of that. Your remarks about time are interesting. Yes, my friend, time shouts as it goes by for me too. Rambam said time is an accident of an accident—like a glint in the color of a jewel. These past years my thoughts have traveled far, since I have been back in prison. I think I traveled the whole ancient world. I can almost imagine the smell of the torch-lit halls of the court of Sennacherib, the throngs in Babylon.

I suppose you are right about the play. But there was a time, you know, when it was not customary to pass judgment on individuals so casually. It's the masses and the masses love a good chase. But, as you suggest, there will be another time and another place—and the play will have another significance altogether.

Life is cheap not because of anyone's contempt for it, but because of the defects of the world. Life is cheap *biologically,* organically. A silly accident is all it takes. A small malfunction—and everything is lost. That is why life is cheap. It is not cheap because of war or because of a decision by this or that kind of man. It is not cheap as a consequence of cruelty. Life takes place in a complex accident.

Fate has taken that form. And that is what perplexes me: The masses enjoy seeing someone lose, especially the ones who fight the hardest.

And so it happens sometimes that history takes one of these turns up a blind alley and everything falls apart and goes to seed. The revelers pass by, drunk on their swollen feelings, in their endless numbers. They soon collapse into slumber and awaken the next day, a little more ashamed. I have never understood how they could look each other in the eyes the next day. But they do.

All creatures under the sun are born with all the knowledge they could ever need. Except man. He has to acquire it. He has to read and listen carefully. He has to stand outside the crowd, and outside his feelings. He has to suffer. To feel pain. He has to sacrifice his personality.

Even the most ignorant of men, even the most coarse, recognize this. But here is the catch: They want to see men who long for knowledge ridiculed. They think we are all born with feelings enough to make us human—as if that were enough and anything more is hubris. They long as the *bestia triumphans* longs and if you listen to them carefully you will hear the storm begin to sing and the swelling of the sea at their backs, waiting for them.

Siamo contenti? Siamo dios ho fatto questa caricatura?

Cheers,
Jack

Dear William Styron,

In 1982 you published a collection of non-fiction writings in a book entitled *This Quiet Dust*. In a chapter titled "Hell Reconsidered" you reviewed the book by Richard Rubenstein, *The Cunning of History*. You imparted your views on the Holocaust. Rubenstein's work argued the thesis that Auschwitz was the culmination of the history of western civilization, which developed out of the civilization of ancient Greece and Rome in the history of slavery. You praised this thesis because of its "serene and Olympian analysis of evil." Then you tell us it is this quality (of the analysis) which probably accounts for the lack of acceptance with which it is met in some quarters. I would like to dwell on this for a moment.

Slavery did not exist in European civilization, if by slavery one means chattel slavery. Otherwise the word is merely being used as a metaphor. Serfdom was not slavery as the term is strictly applied. Slavery in the colonies of Europe (America, for example) was not only a thing of the past but was, at the time of Auschwitz, an organization of labor that *absolutely* contradicted the level of the material forces of production. This is the reason an analysis of "slavery" in Germany during the war is unacceptable. Your analysis pivoted on questions of efficiency and feasibility, and the fact of working slaves to death and putting useless slaves out of their misery. That was not the point, and, despite your doubts in the matter, in the civilized world we have economically eliminated the *possibility* of the slave organization of labor ever coming into existence again, so long as civilization stands.

But the Third Reich (and not merely Auschwitz) was indeed a continuation of the history of western civilization and can indeed be traced back to ancient Greece and Rome. Greece as well as Rome arose on the foundations of a shattered and defeated population. The *institution* of slavery is deeply embedded in the state, because the state came into existence as an instrument to organize and maintain slaves.

In other words, there can be no state without its *essence:* the *institution* of slavery. The modern criminal justice system of the west developed in Rome: out of the foundations of slavery (see the privately published book which has recently appeared in the "prison movement" titled *Prison Slavery* and the book by Bruce Franklin, *Prison Literature*). In ancient Greece the process was the same but not on such a grand scale as in Rome when it became unprofitable for citizens to own multitudes of slaves, when the *latifundias* were going bankrupt and civil disorders were completely out of hand. The proletariat first came into existence at this time. Over this period in Rome the code of criminal procedure was perfected for the first time anywhere. For the first time anywhere in history the state arrogated to itself the right to *prosecute* citizens for offenses against other citizens and their private property. The state assumed the haughty status of the Victim. In a manner of speaking, this is where Auschwitz began. The category of "criminal" came into existence out of that of "slave." Punishment for *crime* became slavery to the state. The state for the first time gathered to itself the right to evaluate the worth of a human being and the power of life or death over anyone within its jurisdiction (borders). The state acted with the force of god over man and over the very geographical terrain on which he stood. This is not simply "Roman law," as the Nazis implied when they stated as one of their aims that they would divest Germany of Roman concepts of jurisprudence. It is the "Aryan state." Rome merely held it together longer than previous Aryan states had been able to do. It was done with a criminal justice system.

The question the Holocaust has posed for western civilization is the justification of the state composed of bodies of armed men. The limits of force are at issue. Auschwitz represents the logical conclusion of the state as a nation-state in its course through history. Had the National Socialist movement been victorious, it would have been the end of the world as we know it. It could even be argued that no scientific progress would have been achieved—not even on the basis of war, up to a limit. It could be argued successfully that productivity would have actually begun a retrograde slide into some nightmare medieval world. The essence of the nation-state is feudalism, a *form* of slavery.

The connection of Auschwitz with slavery is only in that sense valid, and extermination is more closely related historically to the execution of criminals than the dispensibility of slave labor. Those of us who find Rubenstein's account unacceptable for being "serene and Olympian" do so for these reasons. It is cavalier.

If I remember correctly, your position on the "slave question" that once divided this country was that all the unpleasantness that led to pitting white people against each other (the Civil War) could have been avoided with a system of manumission. In other words, if your Southern slaveholding ancestors had devised a justice system (like the Moslem system) whereby individual slaves who were ready to be free men could work their way out of slavery, it would have prevented the Civil War. You wanted, in essence, a just parole system. (Your book on Nat Turner, by the way, only served to illustrate that the slaves were too ignorant to fight for their freedom. It is a book about a marauding band of desperate fugitives in a strange and hostile land and, in my view, a subtle attack on black people and their dignity as a people.)

David Susskind asked a panel on television, "Why are you people interested in the Holocaust?" In your review of Rubenstein's book you related this incident. You tell us you were watching Susskind on television when he said this. You were laying down in darkness, alone with the television. You report that it irritated you—and that Susskind was Jewish and the panel was not Jewish. It irritated you to the point of talking to yourself. You report that you began "murmuring to myself in the dark." You thought it was at least tasteless and that Susskind must have been insensitive to ask such a foolish question. You had your feathers ruffled because, as anybody but a fool would know, Jews were not the only people who were exterminated in the Holocaust. So Susskind's "tasteless" question must have implied that Susskind thought only Jews were exterminated in the Holocaust. Then you began to tick off the names of various nationalities who were also exterminated. You acceded (of course) that more Jews were killed and that they were treated worse, etc. However, it was because non-Jews were exterminated that you felt non-Jews should be interested in the Holocaust. You felt Susskind should have known this.

And you murmured to yourself in the dark. And you record a few of your murmurings in this review of Rubenstein's book. One of them is a fact that belongs in Ripley's *Believe It or Not:* The first people exterminated with Zyklon B gas at Auschwitz were not one thousand Jews but (shout it from the rooftops) one thousand *Russians.* Another statistic: "There were thousands of Poles and Russians and Czechs and Slovenes" who were also exterminated. And "droves of Catholic priests and nuns who were subjected to excruciating and fatal medical experiments," etc.

Another statistic you want us to remember: *"Three-quarters of a million"* people exterminated *"fell into the category which the Nazis termed Aryan. This was at Auschwitz alone. Multitudes of innocent civilians were murdered elsewhere."* And do you imply that Jews were not innocent civilians? And what you do not tell us is that the one thousand Russians were communist commissars (Red Army partisan-organizers). And what you do not tell us is that the Nazis "portrayed" the communist movement as a form of politics brought into existence by Jews. And what you do not tell us is that all people exterminated (partisans, neutrals, liberals, resistance fighters, etc.) were considered to hold "Jewish views" and advance the Jewish "cause." They were held to be Jewish sympathizers and collaborators no matter what their race. *That was the only reason non-Jews were exterminated.* In other words, the non-Jews were exterminated for anti-Semitic reasons. Those who expressed liberal or humanistic views (the tradition we call the Enlightenment) were considered to be tools and dupes of the Jews—whether they helped the Jews deliberately or not.

This is why David Susskind asked why non-Jews are interested in the Holocaust.

I can see why George Steiner, in despair, could recommend silence.

Mein Kampf is the bible of the Nazi movement. *Mein Kampf* organized the National Socialist Party. *Mein Kampf* organized the Third Reich. *Mein Kampf* organized the Nazi military and the Nazi economy. There is a tendency to discount the importance of *Mein Kampf* and to advance the mistaken idea that it was not the final word on all ideological and political questions and policies. *Mein Kampf* singled out Jews in order to attack human rights, democracy, liberal arts, progressive education, individual freedom—and every value we considered enlightened and European. It attacked the whole concept of tolerance and free thought in its attack on Jews. In short, *Mein Kampf* aimed at the annihilation of all civilization through the annihilation of Jews.

In *Mein Kampf* Hitler discussed the low mentality of the masses and he prescribed formulas for translating party objectives into language which would move the masses to do what they wanted them to do (what we call The Big Lie). What the masses understood was ethnic and racial language. The cheap propaganda of a racist nature, handed down in slogans from the party to the rank-and-file, concealed broader ideological aims of the Nazi party. The Nazi party and *Mein Kampf* took up a false concept of race and declared the German Aryan to be superior to all other "races." But it was not the immediate objective in *Mein Kampf* to exterminate and enslave other races—unless it served the Third Reich to do so. Hitler in fact condescendingly praised several "races" in *Mein Kampf,* including Russians. It was Hitler's "theory" that the Jewish people were so ancient their blood had a "disunity." Hitler set out to rid civilization of the Jewish people, and this was a deadly racist aim directed *only* against the Jewish people. Hitler would have destroyed that very civilization in the effort. He in fact openly declared that his aims were barbarian. It is not of paramount importance that Poles, Russians, Czechs, Slovenes, and even Aryans and Catholics were also exterminated. What is important is that *people* were exterminated. And of major importance: *Why* they were exterminated. They were not exterminated because of their race. Only the Jews were.* The others were exterminated because they stood up for freedoms that the Nazis considered "Jewish." They were exterminated for ideological reasons: for anti-Semitic reasons.

You write, "Unlike slavery—which, after all, has had its quixotic defenders—Auschwitz can have no proponents whatever." Your views of slavery, since they are apologetic, could be described as a "quixotic defense." Auschwitz *does* have proponents and you know it. Auschwitz and the Nazi movement is alive in the South and in other parts of the world. It is alive in Europe and America. There are even factions in the schools of penology, with high-placed representatives in the justice system, who are today proponents of Auschwitz. *Mein Kampf* is still the bible of the movement. You may discount these facts all you like, you may refuse to take them seriously, but you must not *deny* that these facts exist. It is your murmuring alone in the dark that should concern everyone, all the more because you do not comprehend what a confession it really was to mention it. I wonder what you will think when you read these lines. The roots of anti-Semitism are ignorance. That ignorance applied to the holy

---

*The Gypsies were the only exception. They were considered "stateless" because they had no peasant classes of farmers. They had no permanent settled life in any country. They were nomadic traders. In the war, they were not allowed to be neutral and in the struggle to exist they were enemies of the Nazi forces. It was not their race *per se* that condemned them. Theoreticians in Germany placed them variously as migrating out of ancient India or ancient Egypt. However, it is my opinion they came into existence on the roads of the great trade-routes during the period when the Silk Road dominated world trade. I am more inclined to place them closer to Persia historically, before the Mongols arose and put an end to the trade-route system and smashed Persia. It could be more than ironic that Styron does not mention the plight of the Gypsies.—J.A.

bible is but one instance of a source of anti-Semitism. But this form of ignorance sets the cultural stage in Christianity for mass movements, just as it does in the Islamic world.

The defense of civilization in the Second World War depended on the defense of the Jews, and we were barely able to succeed. The Holocaust *means* that. The values the Jews take for their own and defend are the values that the best of all other peoples also died for in the Holocaust. The Jews represented all good Europeans. What is most irritating in your "Hell Reconsidered" chapter is that you quote the words of Jewish authorities which suggest that the Jews should not emphasize their own numbers in the Holocaust and that they should instead give at least equal emphasis to the fact that non-Jews also died in the Holocaust. You turn their own words against them. What the Jews say to one another about the Holocaust you want them to say to you. What Susskind wanted to know in his academic question is why non-Jews seem interested in the Holocaust when only Jews are discussing it seriously. In other words, are non-Jews interested in it merely because they are commissioned to write about it or assigned to study it at school? This is what concerned Susskind and what concerns the Jewish authorities you cite without comprehending.

I have never written to you before, nor have I met you. You have never written me and of course you've never met me. But you wrote about me also in *This Quiet Dust* (you take your titles from phrases in famous poems, imitating another bad novelist, Hemingway). I think the original judgment of you as a "literary politicker" is still true today in your habit of name-dropping.

I am now responding to what you wrote about me in *This Quiet Dust* in the chapter titled "Aftermath." Hopefully, no one has heard of the book (since it is not a novel) and so I will necessarily have to write things here you already know but that many readers probably do not know.

I am going to bring you up to date on a few matters.

What we call the McCarthy Era in the early 1950s opened up with a full-scale war on crime in the streets, all centered around an eighteen-year-old young man who had been raised in state orphanages and children's penal institutions in California. He was eventually executed for his writings. He wrote several best-selling books about his life, and he stands today as the one who started the modern prison reform movement which not only reformed the California prison system but reformed our whole view of prisons all across America. His writings started reforms that continue to this day.

Caryl Chessman was a poor white self-educated prisoner, and no lawyer could safely defend him without ruining his career, due to the right-wing publicity generated by Senator McCarthy. Chessman's crime was simple rape. There was a park in Los Angeles popularly called Lover's Lane. At night, couples would park their cars at different places in Lover's Lane, undo parts of their clothing, and perform coitus, either in the back seat or in the front seat of the car. If a policeman were to venture upon them copulating, they would be ordered to get dressed and step out of the car. They say most of the people who went there to copulate in their cars were betraying their spouses. None of them were young adults. Most of them did not want to go to the expense of renting a hotel room for the night. Local teenage boys prowled through the park and had adventures sneaking up to the cars unnoticed and watching the adults copulate. It was a local custom for teenage boys to prowl mischievously through Lover's Lane at night.

I will assume for the sake of avoiding arguments that Caryl Chessman was guilty. Caryl Chessman was accused of this: He was accused of prowling Lover's Lane (nowhere else) and interrupting people in the act of copulating, ordering the male to step out of the car, then slipping down his trousers and mounting the already-prone female for a few minutes. Period. All of the victims were generally between age thirty and forty.

The way he did it became his trademark, what the police call *modus operandi*. Eighteen-year-old Caryl carried a large flashlight on those nights and shined it in the window on the couple. In a bass, commanding voice he would order the surprised couple to stop. Then he ordered the man to step out of the car. All through this he kept the blinding light of the flashlight on their faces. No one could ever positively identify him. When the man stepped out, fumbling with his clothes, Caryl would order him to stand behind the car and wait. Then he would take the man's place and complete the act of coitus he had interrupted. Caryl Chessman imitated the *modus operandi* of the Los Angeles police. He was accused of doing this six times and on one occasion varying the *modus operandi* by having the woman climb into his car. Caryl was of medium height, slight of build, and smooth-cheeked. He was not a physical brute. He was eighteen years old, a teenager.

Caryl Chessman never brandished a weapon; he did not strike or verbally threaten anyone with violence. He became known in the massive, lurid publicity as the "Red Light Bandit" because, in conformity with the police, he had a small red light on the dashboard of his car so that it glowed like a police light through the window. In those days in California, rape *could* be punishable by execution in the gas chamber. I do not believe that in the whole history of California any other white man was ever executed for rape. That was reserved for Hispanics and blacks; but even this had become a thing of the past.

You demanded his execution because after Caryl Chessman's first book became widely read and popular in America and Europe, support groups in Italy and France (and other places) organized with large support groups in America and signed petitions asking the Governor of California to commute his death sentence to life imprisonment. They also petitioned the courts to let Caryl live, if only in a prison cell.

Using your prestige as a hot new novelist (in Europe they mistake them for intellectuals and men of conscience), you wrote an open letter to the press informing Europe that Caryl Chessman was found guilty at a fair trial and that the appeal judges should be supported in their decision to execute Chessman. Eighteen-year-old Chessman did not have a lawyer at his trial. He defended himself clear through his appeals. He was his own lawyer to the end. Chessman was perceptive and brilliant and the courts resented this.

In *This Quiet Dust* you tell us, after the fact, that you did it for patriotic reasons. You did not want it said in France (in particular) that American law and order could have made a mistake. You gave one more reason. Never having met him, you wrote that you heard that Caryl Chessman was arrogant, in the sense of his *personality*. No other reason. The black-listing and Red-baiting to purge America of unpatriotic writers and artists was in progress. You proved your loyalty. You were a red-blooded American. You defended your country before France. That was the real reason. You picked a helpless man to "prove" this on, not another novelist or artist who could fight you back.

Caryl Chessman was not an intellectual; he was not a socialist or a communist. He held no political views. He was not another Jean Genet—he was not eccentric sexually. He was not a thief, nor had he a record of violence. He was not boastful or in any way proud. His books were straightforward and written only to record information. Where the expression of an attitude was necessary he was usually humble. He wrote about juvenile penal institutions in California. Period.

Then with the McCarthy Era safely in the past, you wrote a single article in *Esquire* magazine (in 1962) asking for the commutation of a death-row inmate's death penalty. The prisoner's lawyers were in the midst of appealing his death sentence in the state of Connecticut, which had seldom carried out the death penalty. His chances of having his sentence commuted to life imprisonment were almost certain. The man was considered to have so low an intelligence as to be moronic. As a matter of due process, his sentence was commuted to life imprisonment.

Now you step forward and tell us in *This Quiet Dust* that you "saved a man's life." If you saved that man's life, then it follows by your own "reasoning" that you were responsible for the unconscionable state-murder of Caryl Chessman—Chessman who, as a writer, contributed more to America and did more productive writing than you, in your entire life, could have ever accomplished. If you were in his shoes you would never have had the stuff to be a writer.

The man who you boast of having rescued was tried for murder and sentenced to death and freely admitted his crimes. But he described his intentions as good. Caryl Chessman argued eloquently up to the day he died in the gas chamber that he was not guilty of simple rape. It was a fact that all the evidence against him was circumstantial. The man you supported was caught quite literally red-handed.

He was older than Chessman. He had a carpenter's hammer. He approached an elderly woman by a parking lot. He reached for her purse and she would not release it. She screamed. He wrestled with her and the old woman fought back. She would not release her purse. He hit her in the face with his hammer. She screamed. She was drawing attention so he hit her again with the hammer. To silence her. She fell to her knees. Screaming. She would not release her purse. He coldly hit her again with the hammer. On the head. She screamed. He hit her again. On the head. Again and again. Until she was silent. Dead. He dragged her body behind a parked car, opened the trunk, picked her up, and stuffed her in it. Then he closed the trunk and nervously stole away with her purse.

The court believed the man was a moron because at his trial, on the witness stand, he tried to explain that he killed her to stop her from screaming because *it bothered him to see an old woman in pain.*

I want to be clear that no one was insane enough to believe his stated motives. It was really the bare fact that he could think of nothing else (and that he thought it was convincing) which demonstrated his low mentality. Yet the man was repentant, and sincerely so.

He finally won a parole. Per normal procedures he was taken away from the main prison and placed in a minimum security prison facility to await the day of his parole. A few weeks before he was to be paroled he walked away from the minimum security facility. He next appeared with an automobile antenna sharpened to a point as a weapon, forced his way into a house in a suburb, and interrupted a woman and her two children at the breakfast table. He kidnapped the young woman and her two children and proceeded down a road with them in the woman's car. At some point he stopped the car and raped the woman in the presence of her children. He later abandoned them in the car and fled on foot. The woman, of course, called the police.

Again, he exhibited his intelligence by telling the court, after his capture, that the woman either offered herself sexually to him or submitted willingly. He was nonetheless convicted of the rape. Needless to say, had his story been true, why did she call the police?

This may be elementary to "dear Watson" but it completely loses you, a famous novelist. In *This Quiet Dust* you do not hesitate to sail into character defamation of an innocent victim by telling us all that you think it was true, that the rape victim was (at least) willing. You also tell us that he bludgeoned the old woman to death (and concealed her body) because he was sensitive to her pain.

Anyone who could support you in these things would have to be as defective as you—I say "defective" because I am not referring to moral turpitude but the processes of *reason,* logic. You take your readers for fools. You seem not to want to appear to be a real liberal who is against execution *in principle.* This must be why you offer up these "Alice in Wonderland" reflections, to make yourself appear "humanitarian."

Caryl Chessman never kidnapped a victim. He never broke into people's homes and confronted them. He never threatened anyone with a weapon. He never raped a victim in the presence of anyone else, much less children. He never killed anyone.

—What has all this to do with me?

In *This Quiet Dust* you compare me with your death-row inmate and then you tell us that "manslaughter is a greater atrocity than rape"—as if rape, not the murder of an old woman for her purse, were the issue. Although innocent, I was convicted of manslaughter.

Manslaughter is distinguished from murder because it involves an element of self-defense, as any lawyer or legislator could tell you. Anyone convicted of manslaughter has convinced the jury that the crime began as an act of self-defense.

There is no element of self-defense in the crime of rape. There is no extenuating element.

Society (the law) has always treated rape as a "greater atrocity" than manslaughter. The laws against rape carry harsher penalties than laws against manslaughter for that reason.

In *This Quiet Dust* you make references to your Christian views in condemning me. But what you call the "Old Testament" set aside cities in the lands of Israel for sanctuary and judgment of those fleeing accusations of manslaughter. Nowhere else in barbarian antiquity was a distinction made between murder and manslaughter. The law of blood ruled, the vendetta. Even if it was known that you killed a man accidentally, his relatives were bound by duty to kill you or otherwise seek vengeance.

Powerful families negotiated these matters, but a powerless man from a powerless family was at the mercy of everyone. The refusal to recognize the distinction between murder and manslaughter is a rejection of civilization. It is lawless. Barbarian.

But you wrote that you find rape to be less of an "atrocity" than manslaughter. I think this is interesting, that in *your* opinion manslaughter is a more serious crime.

And yet, after twelve years in a cell in San Quentin's death-row, you wanted Caryl Chessman to be put to death for rape, committed when he was eighteen years old.

It is interesting that you confess doing this to Chessman for patriotic reasons. And during the McCarthy Era when the careers and the loyalty of writers and artists were placed in question by the right-wing factions of the Republican Party: *This* you do not mention in *This Quiet Dust*. Why?

Who was the better "American," Mr. Styron? You or Caryl Chessman?

What have you done for society to make it better? What have you ever risked? As far as I know, you have never in your writings confronted anyone who has the power to respond intellectually.

I have developed a response to circumstances of danger that is probably more marked in me than in others whose life might resemble mine. What I mean by danger is not mainly physical danger, although at one time it was. What I mean is danger in the sense of being tricked or deceived into doing something I would not ordinarily do. The drive for self-preservation has always dominated my life. That is why I have never developed faculties for revenge. I do not even know what it is. I have been too preoccupied defending myself and having to account for myself. Revenge undoes the drive for self-preservation, as anyone who has fought alone for a long time knows. It is too costly. The impulses of self-defense are really only what we call *taste*. I think this is true even in the sense Kant used the term. Aesthetic sensitivity is indeed sharpened and developed as a result of personal self-defense of one's feelings and one's inmost responses to life. I think this is what constitutes the ground of higher culture.

This criticism of you is not literary revenge. It is written in anticipation of other "critics" similar to you who might rise up again. I have merely addressed myself to you as to a whole trend. —Unlike you, I mean nothing personal. I am not vindictive. I do not want you executed or placed in prison for your views.

It is my understanding the Ministry of Culture in France made the mistake of honoring you, along with other American writers, as a literary man of conscience.

For what it is worth, I demand here, in this letter, that the Ministry of Culture apologize to the other American writers for the insult.

There.

Cordially,
Jack Henry Abbott

Dear Jerzy,

It has been a while now since the evening we finally met at Il Molinas. Of course we had corresponded for years over many subjects. Somehow it is easier to remember our arguments, all of them over communism. You had fled the Soviet Union alone when you were eighteen years old and I went to prison at the same age. My memories of the arguments have become absurd and have faded away into lack of comprehension. My arguments had no reality because I had no experience. It was the *idea* I think I fought for. And I was exasperated that you denounced it. It is odd that the only thing that gave the idea importance or validity was *optimism*. Without optimism the idea could not even have substance.

I was moved by your first book because the Red Army was portrayed in a good light and because of the misunderstandings that met the main protagonist throughout the book. The protagonist was a twelve-year-old boy, who was rescued by the Red Army. In those days (1973?) I knew very little about Poland and east Central Europe. Before I got out of prison I had begun thinking seriously about it. In the federal prison system there are prisoners from all parts of the world and I always made a point of getting to know them and engaging them in conversations about their countries. I knew a Yugoslavian Croatian. A Hungarian from Budapest. An Albanian. And many more. All the Poles I met were born in America.

The partisan fighters throughout east Central Europe during World War II always seemed to me to typify the ideal of the industrial European revolutionary. Of course that was then. But I wanted to talk to you about life in Poland and, perhaps, Moscow. Poland was once the center of European civilization. It was once the greatest among the European nations. Its frontiers once stretched from Odessa on the Black Sea clear up to the coastlands of the North Sea. The borders east and west were never stable. Poland served as the buffer between Europe and the Asiatic and Islamic worlds. Poland defended Western Europe and protected its way of life. That seems to be a historical destiny which Poland cannot escape.

I often wondered, in thinking about modern Poland, what weakened Poland so that it was divided within itself and became prey to Russia and other nations. Rembrandt painted a portrait of a Polish noble astride his horse, decked out in armor. It is called *The Rider* and it sits today over the mantelpiece of the fireplace on the ground floor of the Frick Museum in Manhattan. I viewed it when I was in Manhattan but my interest centered around the poise and graceful lines of the horse. A scholarly friend, however, explained to me that the rider was a Polish noble and that experts date him by his dress as appearing at the zenith of Polish civilization. At some point in Polish history its higher culture began to crumble—and I would say that around the mid-nineteenth century it had been pulled to the ground and torn apart by many ethnic differences—the same ignorant masses who tortured and abused that boy in your first novel. It is ironic that the Red Army did not punish the individuals who committed the crimes against him and yet lifted him out of their midst.

The little I understand now of the struggle taking place in Poland tells me that among the Poles there is a struggle taking place to restore a higher culture and that Poland is beginning to embrace its historical destiny and confront a Russia that is now looming over Western Europe and has become a greater threat today than ever before. I think the nations of Western Europe must eventually dissolve their petty pride and unite politically as one force and deal with Russia if they are to continue to exist. The question of Poland's right to self-determination is an all-European question and if it is not seen in this light nothing can stop European culture from vanishing.

But this struggle in Poland, on the one hand within the masses and on the other hand against Soviet domination, is a struggle that could decide where European civilization will have a place in the world in the future. If Solidarity is defeated, and the struggle for culture is lost, the consequences for all of Western Europe could be devastating.

Some creature I have never spoken to in my life, but had the misfortune to be seated at the same table with for dinner at someone's home, has invented long tales about conversations I have never held with him. He has gone into print with one of those tales saying that I discussed Poland with him. This is not true at all. I have never spoken to him. If there was any substance to it, it would have stemmed from something said that evening by an old man originally from Poland who fought in the Resistance. He had just returned from a visit to Poland and was discussing the food shortages engineered by the puppet Soviet government in Poland as a means to turn the masses against the Solidarity movement. As I recall, the creature who told the tall tales about me had not even been in the room during the conversation but was discussing perfumes with our host's fashionable wife in the next room.

I wanted to tell you this as the best way of setting aside our past disputes. I have thought about you these intervening years and the bitterness that may or may not have resulted. It is true that I did not follow your advice that evening. I do not think I really knew how to. At the time I was not aware of the *whole situation.* I was only aware of possibly *particular* situations. I was not alert and I did not realize the full danger. I did not realize the full import of stepping from one world into another. I think, since I know quite a lot about you, that you know what I mean. I never had an inkling of what it was until I found myself alone and almost penniless in Mexico (without even enough knowledge of the language to feed myself), where it confronted me in its extreme form.

In any case, this is to wish you well and send my best.

In friendship,
Jack

Epistle to Paul

March 1986

Dear Paul,

Mama was small but not thin. All my life she told me she was "thirty-six years old," even when she was fifty years of age. And she could have passed for thirty-six. She carried her age well. She had thick black hair, lustrous as the wings of a raven. When she died at the age of sixty-one, it was just as black and lustrous as ever. When I was a small boy, sitting at her feet, she would let her hair down and it would fall like a long, heavy cloak down her back and along the floor. Her hair was longer than her height, so long and thick I could hide behind it. She would toss her head as she stood over me and her hair would fall around me. And we would shout with laughter. My memory of her is good.

When I was a boy, part of the Mormon teaching was that the "mark of Cain" was passed on through the bloodline of one of Noah's sons, named Ham. This was their interpretation of the bible. According to the Mormon account, the Chinese and the Africans were blood descendants of Ham. The Mormons believed that the blacks and the Chinese displayed the mark of Cain in the pigmentation of their skin. Anyone who had the mark of Cain could join the Mormon church but could never rise through the ranks of the church hierarchy. A male, for example, was barred from the priesthood. In the state of Utah no white person, whatever his religion, could marry a non-white person. But non-whites could interbreed freely with other non-white races. The Mormons went beyond mere laws against miscegenation.

Justice Warren abolished laws against miscegenation in the early sixties—and (coincidentally) the same day God told someone in the Mormon Temple that it was now okay to let all races marry white people.

The Mormon God is obviously a law-abiding American citizen, among other divine attributes.

While my mother was a Mormon convert, she could not be what the Mormons refer to as an "active Mormon." The Mormons believed that if non-whites lived right in this world, when they died they could be white in heaven. White was the Mormon redemptive reward for non-whites. My mother was the only person who had the mark of Cain in her church ward.

While Mama could attend services on Sunday, for some reason she chose to stay home but insisted that I attend. I was in the priesthood. My mother never explained to me the racial doctrines of the Mormon religion. I do not know today if she knew it was part of the religion (and not merely community culture).

One of my mother's married names was "Crawshaw." She was buried under this name. Her family name was "Jung" (today the new roman is "Chung"). At the time of her death she was living alone in a pretty attic apartment under the eaves of a three-story house. It was in a nice residential district on the east side of town. In the spring and summer, the world was full of treetops. The children playing in the yards and all the houses and the hubbub on the ground seemed to be a world behind glass whose inhabitants could not conceive of what it is to be watched. The breezes that passed along the foot of the mountains that surround the east side of town were stirred up by currents as steady and winding as the Yellow River, making the leaves dance. It made the nooks and shingles whisper and sometimes sing. Her bed was in an alcove just off her living room. It was a brass, fancy-wrought bed with a high, firm mattress. The bed stood against the wall. In the wall there was a window. The window-sill was flush with the top of her bed. One could roll a ball smoothly across her bed and it would cross the windowsill and drop thirty feet to the ground. The hinges on the window frame were attached to the *top* of the window casement. On the windowsill a small eye screw secured the latch-hook attached to the wooden frame of the window to keep it closed. The window opened outward and it was kept open only by propping it up with a stick. There was no chain or stay or any means of holding the window open. My mother would lean forward on her knees on her bed and hold the window out with one hand. With her other hand, she placed the end of the stick, about one foot in length, against a ledge in the windowsill. With one hand she would then draw the frame of the window against the protruding end of the stick, which she held in place with her other hand. Then she would release the stick. The window would stay open, resting on the end of the stick. The window was four feet wide and about three feet high. Opening it involved both hands in the task, as she leaned forward on her knees.

In the month of June (1964), when the summer heat is on the rise to its crescendo in July, at about three o'clock in the morning, my mother in her long nightgown fell out the window. Her body fell on the wooden pickets of a fence and came to rest on the ground a few feet from the house. The occupants of the basement apartment telephoned the ambulance. She died at a hospital about four hours later from massive internal hemorrhaging. She was sixty-one years of age when she died.

The newspapers and the death reports described it as a household accident. I was twenty years old at the time. I had been in prison two years by then, for issuing a check against insufficient funds. I was in disciplinary isolation for punishment at the time. Salt Lake City was twenty-five miles away. Besides my sister, my mother was virtually my only living relative. I was not allowed to attend my mother's funeral, not because I was in the hole but because the warden and the rest of the guards wanted it to be a lesson to me. When my mother died it made me cry and they saw me express something more than anger. They had a problem punishing me. They punished me by not allowing me to attend her funeral. I do not remember how many days I wept. I do not remember when I stopped. They taunted me over her death.

My mother was buried in the main Mormon graveyard of the city cemetery. Just before I was released to the halfway house to await my parole in 1981, I discovered that my mother's coffin had been exhumed and removed to the Chinese section of the graveyard. I also learned that there was no tombstone or marker of any kind on her grave or the grave of her father (my grandfather). And I learned that no one knew where the grave sites of my mother and her father were. I had discovered all this in a discussion with my sister while we were planning the trip from the prison to the airport. I wanted to stop at my mother's grave before I boarded the plane for New York.

My sister went to the caretaker's offices and, after a search through records, she was given a map of the graveyard indicating where the two graves were located. My grandfather was in the "old Chinese section."

In my cell I designed matching tombstones in black marble and I composed inscriptions for both of them, with inlays of their portraits. I had decided to someday (and very soon) come back and gather their remains and take them to China personally, for their final resting place. My grandfather's clan was somewhere in Canton province.

My sister met me at the prison gates and drove me from the prison to the graveyard. It was June, the same month and season in which my mother had died seventeen years before. The graveyard was at the foot of the mountain and it was silent and empty and full of trees and winding lanes. My sister stopped the car and walked ahead of me among the tombstones, all inscribed in Chinese letters. She stopped beside what resembled a small stone fireplace. There was a depression in the grass beside it and she told me that this was where my mother was buried. The tombstones I designed had not been finished and so my mother's tombstone was not in place, nor was there a marker. Then my sister took me up a rise on the side of the mountain and out onto an area that resembled a golf course. She walked ahead of me, stopped, turned, spread her arms, and, letting her gaze fall around her, told me my grandfather was buried somewhere in this area. I did not know what to say. I watched.

We returned to the car and drove straight to the airport.

She sent me photographs of the finished tombstones, in place at the graves, a couple of months after I had been returned to prison. My mother was buried beside either a Buddhist or Confucian incense-burner (once called a "sacrificial altar"). The sea had cast her up again. May a curse hang over the Mormons until the mountain she is buried against falls across the whole valley.

It sickens me to rehash my origins so I will be as brief and simple as possible about this. I was kept in foster homes in Texas until around the age of three. My parents were reunited in Utah after the war. My father was in an Army hospital in Utah with malaria, contracted in the Pacific Theatre of the war. He was in the U.S. Air Force for over five years. I lived with them for a little less than one year before they were divorced. Then I began living in foster homes in Utah.

My father was about thirty-five years old when I was born. He came from an old Texas family. I believe they were Baptists.

My mother had converted to the Mormon religion before I was born. She was forty-one years old when I was born. My mother was born in

Tennessee, the daughter of wealthy Chinese. They owned businesses there. She was raised partly in China and partly in the United States. I believe most of her years until she was about eighteen years of age were spent in China. She was born in 1903. I was her last child, her seventh (after six daughters). She lost all her children, except my sister and me.

I believe I was four years old when they were divorced. The Child Welfare Department placed my sister and me in a series of temporary foster homes. Our mother would not allow us to be adopted. I was never abused as a child in any of these foster homes, although I believe my sister was mistreated in at least one of them.

In those days, most of what is today part of metropolitan Salt Lake City was farm country. So we lived both in farming communities and in the "city."

There was one family we passed through regularly and spent most of our time with until I was about nine or ten years old. The father of this family was a Mormon patriarch, with at least four wives and fifty-four children. My sister and I were the only outsiders they ever took in, so my mother could visit us on a regular basis. They were of the original Mormon stock that emigrated to the Territories from upstate New York in the early nineteenth century. They were observant, orthodox Mormons. They are mentioned in the book by Dorothy Solomon (under false names) titled, *In My Father's House.*

For the sake of discretion, I will call my "foster patriarch" Uncle Albert. He was sent to the old territorial prison, along with about twenty other patriarchs in 1944 for practicing "plural marriage" (polygamy).

While Utah was still a territory the Mormons went to war against the U.S. government and, of course, lost. Utah was the only territory that was forced to become a state and in which white settlers were forced to join the Union. The Mormons were forced to abandon their polygamist marriage practices, which were the main source of social cohesion in Utah, if not the whole West. The religious leaders were divided over this issue and those who went along with the terms of the U.S. Senate of course prevailed. The rest became fugitives, persecuted by what is today the Mormon establishment. Yet they do not denounce the establishment and they live with the hope that one day it will lift the persecution. They are the only people in the Western world who practice polygamy.

This form of society was abolished by Germanic rulers around the tenth century to drive the Moslems and Jews from European lands. It was the first anti-Semitic custom introduced into Western Europe. The legend of Don Juan is actually an exposition of the ill effect of man set free from polygamist obligations to the opposite sex, an exposition of the influence of what later developed into Germanic romanticism, best illustrated in the suicide of young Werther, the main protagonist in Goethe's novella.

At any rate, in the latter part of the 1950s, Uncle Albert was sent to prison a second time for practicing his religion. His wives had separate households, in separate locations, and he took proper care of everyone, holding religious meetings inside the home, etc.

The children, when the persecutions grew, were drilled in ways to escape from the police and to hide inside the house, to be careful not to talk of any religious matters to outsiders, etc. I too was drilled in this.

This was my earliest relation to Christianity and to Mormonism—my original relation to religion. I must add that while the state prison is full of establishment Mormons, I have never seen or heard of an orthodox Mormon in prison for criminal activity. The only orthodox Mormons sent to prison are patriarchs, for religious reasons having explicitly to do with what they call "plural marriage."

When I was eight years of age I was baptized in the Tabernacle, next to the Temple in Salt Lake City, under the name of "Rufus." ("Jack" is a nickname I have been called all my life. It is not my "Christian name.") The age of eight is the age of reason for Mormons. I was later ordained a "deacon" (servant) in what the Mormons called "the Aaronic Priesthood." I was baptized for the dead in the Temple. I should also remark that as a naif, I had an awful tendency to take solemn matters seriously. I was taken to the house of a Seer and my fortune was told and transcribed. This is, of course, illegal.

At about this age my sister and I returned to live permanently with our mother—and I began being sent to juvenile delinquent quarters for vandalistic juvenile behavior. My sister never had brushes with the law. She was three years older than I, and at age fifteen she married and began raising her own family.

My mother was religious and filled me with Old Testament stories. I never saw her angry or heard her use harsh language. As a Mormon, she did not smoke tobacco, use any form of alcoholic beverage, or drink coffee—all these are forbidden of Mormons. She wanted me to be a good Mormon. My reason revolted.

Before I was sent to the State Industrial School for Boys, I was removed from my mother and sent to two more foster homes. I escaped from each of them in turn. The last time, I was apprehended in my travels from a foster home near the Idaho border on my way back to Salt Lake City. I was twelve years old, close to thirteen.

But before I had gone to my last foster home, a sculptor had taken me in for a few months, a white-haired old man named Arvard Fairbanks. He had a large studio on the campus of the University of Utah. I was his apprentice. The Child Welfare Department thought I could do well, and Arvard wanted a boy to train, since his own sons had entered professions and had no interest in sculpture. Arvard was over sixty years of age and was trained in Greece. We would go to his studio every morning and work alone together all day. I don't recall him ever speaking to me except to explain the craft of sculpturing. He was a quiet, comfortable man. I liked him very much. He and his wife were both Mormons and were personal friends of David O. McKay, the then-president of the established Mormon church. Subsequently I was in the home of the president and his wife when Arvard visited with them. I knew them when I was a child.

My relation to children my own age was flawed. The children of Uncle Albert were the exception. They were my brothers and sisters. I loved them. But my relation to other children was always disrupted when they discovered I was different racially, that I had Chinese blood in my veins. They had a way of jesting that cut me deeply. It set me apart and, subsequently, I stood in the ranks of the "tough kids" and the Mexican-Americans. Of course this period was the 1950s and the times affected Utah youth as well. It was the generation of juvenile rebels.

When I was sent to the Industrial School for Boys, I developed a life-long hatred of religion, particularly (of course) the established Mormon religion. The Industrial School for Boys was not a nice place, but no one could expect the authorities to admit it, so it is pointless to go into. It has been reformed since I was there. The attendance of religious services each Sunday was mandatory at the Industrial School then. And each Sunday I was placed in the hole for refusing to attend. After services I was released from isolation, so I only spent several hours in the hole each Sunday on account of religion. I refused to go to services and was placed in isolation all the time I was there. It was during this time that I began reading serious literature. My mother visited me and filled my needs to read.

The biggest things in my life over these years were my literary interests in all that the "beatniks" of Greenwich Village were doing and writing, the Cuban Revolution, which I followed like a fanatic ("Dollars for Castro" was the main slogan, and the American establishment supported the Rebels at that time), and the trial of Adolf Eichmann, which I watched on television and never quite believed at the time because of the unspeakable things that were said and that I could not comprehend—what Arendt described with the phrase "the banality of evil."

The writings and doings of the beatniks in the 1950s were perceived by me as culture that cut across all differences between people. I realize today my instinct was right.

I had never thought much about any of this until recently, while I was trying to sort out the sources of some of my misunderstandings and some of the things that were presuppositions that I had never realized a need to examine before.

At some time in my early childhood I remember having asked someone what country Jesus came from and what race he was. And I still remember the reply, although I have forgotten the occasion and who told me this. But I was told Jesus was one of the last of an ancient tribe of people who lived "like communists, except fairly" and that they died off as a race of people shortly after Jesus was born. I was told this extinct tribe lived in a desert (the reference was to the Essenes, of course). Of the Jews I was told they were a religious sect that rejected the New Testament, therefore angering certain kinds of Christians. I was never exposed in experience to any anti-Jewish talk. I did not know they existed outside Europe.

In the Christian world a man can join and disengage from any sect he cares to. He can be a Baptist one day and a Protestant the next day. I thought Judaism was one of these sects as well—i.e., that one could be a Jew one day and a Baptist the next day.

* * *

A sense of another world, the whole spectrum of what we call "religion," does not impose itself on man externally but comes from within. It is *suffering* that comes from without, not religion. It is a biological necessity, rooted in the same intuitions that tell us there is a world of microbes and atoms, an invisible world with only a mediated relation to experience. The way death looms over human consciousness, the *fundamental* fact that human consciousness always and instinctively infers causation, the certainty that there exist archetypes in the unconscious, the "fact" that man has always created the conditions of his own existence, the "fact" that there never has been a human society without religious convictions—all this and more points to a mystery in man's origins and destiny that has very little to do with any other form of life on this planet (as we know it).

I have always known this, even when I was a Marxist. Human existence is so exceptional, so deeply aberrant and abnormal, that this conclusion is inescapable. It is a shattering *perception,* the weight of which can dim the reason and obliterate sanity. It is with this perception one must master his emotions and his reason.

There are higher intellectual faculties than reason. It is the human alone who has a creative *form* of consciousness. By the word "form" I mean to say that man's consciousness takes place in the context of reconstructing or recreating the entire world around him, based on painful estrangement from his essence. The less knowledge he has, the more susceptible he is to trickery and the more susceptible he is to his desires and emotions. Emotions can grip the reason and create gods and spirits, create occult and mystic causes in ignorant longing. (There is an island in the Pacific where ignorant people worship an airplane, for instance.)

Marx referred to this trick of desire and ignorance when he described what he called "the fetishistic characters of commodity production," wherein the commodity market imposes itself on the mind so that man believes the world of commodities is part of the natural order, which he can no more control than the seasons. Ignorance sits the world on its head.

So there are as many religions as there are kinds of ignorance—an endless indeterminate number. It is a weakness of the will (the instrument of the intelligence) to surrender to ignorance. Ignorant people, like stoics (and mules), at best "think" stubbornness is an expression of the will. Or that it is a willingness to subjugate.

I have spent my life trying to overcome my ignorance. I never surrendered to religion (the ignorance of others imposed by quantum force, numbers). I never suffered from the degree of ignorance and isolation that bends men's knees and brings them to "the cross"—until my return to prison.

I am not going into what happened to me upon my return. And by this I mean what has its source and origins outside prison. What was done to me in prison by both the authorities and the inmates is something else I will not discuss. Those who were involved know very well the truth of what happened. And they know they have overwhelmed me with numbers alone.

But it has lost its significance to me now.

But, as remarked above, the *basis* of religious need comes from within and is biological. This has been remarked upon by many men (Nordau among them). It is generally felt as man's separation from a prior state of perfection. This is true descriptively of every kind of religion. The external and specific circumstances which make this intuition particularly acute and painful give birth to particular religions—all involving the intervention of a god in the laws of nature, which is only explained by ideas that transcend nature (metaphysical ideas). In a word, it is through man's ignorance and pain these external religions are constructed.

Whatever may be the secret of man's exceptional condition on this planet, we may never uncover that secret by succumbing to pain and ignorance, represented in an external religion, to assuage the suffering (however severe) from what is described as exile from a condition of perfection.

Even Marx wrote that religion is the general theory of this world, its encyclopedic compendium, its logic in popular form, its spiritual point d'honneur, its enthusiasm, its moral sanction, its solemn complement, and its universal basis of consolation and justification. Criticism has plucked the *imaginary flowers* on the chain not in order that man shall continue to bear that chain without fantasy or consolation but so that he can *throw off* the chain—and pluck the living flower.

Religion has always been used as an instrument to attack others, used for mob violence and for the conquering of political power. It lends itself perfectly to abuse by religious leaders or "leaders" in general who conjure with the religious beliefs of people (i.e., their special brand of ignorance). This is why a critique of religion is even necessary.

* * *

I was in transit to Marion Prison (at the Springfield Medical Center), when I began, for the first time in my life, to seek consolation in religion— very quietly, I read the New Testament. But I was *convinced* before I read it and I was convinced because, at the time, I never understood the forces directed against me from all sides to destroy me and to make life too difficult to live.

Here were my circumstances: I was in D-Unit (10 Building), and I was kept in a cell on the ground floor by the end of the cellhouse. This area is reserved for inmates who are under special restriction (the authorities deny it) and are the most subject to violence by guards. While I had access to a telephone (for reasons assured by my lawyer), I was only allowed the use of a pencil stub about two inches in length. It was replaced daily. I was allowed five books in my cell, which I could exchange when a new book arrived in the mail. A guard penciled over my name: "EXTREMELY DANGEROUS" in bold, black crayon across my door (which was a steel door—not a barred door). Outside visitors on tour through D-Unit were paraded past my door to leer at me through a window, at unexpected times. My cell was five feet wide and about ten feet in length. It was lit by a yellow light bulb. Every morning a bevy of guards took me from my cell and ordered me to walk to the showers (in handcuffs) while they mocked me, reading aloud passages I had written about them in my book. Inmates stood at their doors and shouted death threats in the midst of this. At any other time, let me note, any inmate who was even heard stirring in his cell was attacked by guards.

I had written a letter to the local federal judge contesting being returned to Marion Prison, and the judge had ordered that I be held at Springfield until the matter was litigated in a small courtroom inside the institution. I made several appearances before the judge in this courtroom, and on each occasion the guards escorted me there in this manner: My hands were handcuffed behind my back. Leg irons were attached to my ankles, preventing me from walking normally. Then the two guards would take me into the main prison corridor, teeming with inmates. Then, as we proceeded through this corridor (about the length of a city block), the guards would suddenly walk fast and stay about twenty yards in front of me, while I struggled in vain to keep up with them. It is not unusual for inmates to be attacked and killed when they are chained up in this manner and "escorted" through crowds of hostile inmates.

I was fortunate because no one recognized me.

It went on for nine months.

It was under conditions of this nature I began studying Christianity. It is pointless to add that the guards as well as the inmates were Christians, despite Christian protestations that they are not "true Christians." Neither I personally nor history knows of any other Christianity.

No less a Christian thinker than Kierkegaard has noted that Christendom cannot be "attacked" by pointing out that Christians contradict Christianity in their everyday lives—because everyone says they are not "true Christians." It is a hypocritical religion and, except for a very few, the vast majority are almost *proud* of the fact they do not practice their religion. These people are profoundly ignorant and mean and demonstrate it by hatching up ideas about "sins" that do not exist—and attaching them to "sermons" to terrorize their puny desires.

When I was younger I sincerely believed they were insane.

The religion of Christianity assimilated some of the symbols of the arch-Gentile religion revolving around the very emotional Dionysian mysteries of ancient Greece—where Dionysus is crucified and comes back to life three days later, etc. The initiates of this religion ate pieces of his flesh and drank of his blood, etc.

It appeals to something very deep in the unschooled psyche. It reminds me of the earlier cults of Ba'al worshipers in ancient Israel. I have often wondered if the Greeks descended from these people when Assyria dispersed the tribes.

But at the risk of appearing to "snivel," for your information let me tell you about Christianity in D-Unit (at Springfield Medical Center).

Every Sunday a fundamentalist preacher would appear in the middle of the floor. All the food slots in the cell doors were opened up, so we could not avoid hearing his preaching.

He preached to us how to behave like Christians—to be meek, to forgive, etc. A good 90 percent of the inmates had been beaten routinely in their cells by guards, not to mention the inhuman treatment in other areas.

Springfield is in the center of the so-called "Bible Belt" territory of America. They like to delude themselves that *they* are America's "backbone."

Preachers carry a lot of clout there. But all those preachers have never once tried to prevail upon the guards to be humane. In fact they encourage them to behave the way they behave. Then "ask" inmates to forgive *them* their sins.

One day I glanced out the window of my door at the preacher. There was usually a different one each Sunday. All these "Bible Belt" preachers are self-appointed. This fellow was big, burly. He was an off-duty guard. When he noticed I was watching him he turned red and lost his train of "thought." He sputtered a few more words, then closed his bible and left. He was about thirty-seven or thirty-eight years old.

This man had been one of a half-dozen guards who had (years before) attacked me in my cell. I had witnessed him involved in criminal assaults on helpless men—physically weak and broken, meek men.

And he was preaching.

That is a very Christian custom. Before I left I saw him up to his same old nonsense, with the same old gang, beating up an inmate who was strapped to a steel pallet.

A representative from the so-called Christian Prison Ministry came to my cell. This is how it happened: The guards had passed a telephone into my cell, and I was speaking to my lawyer. Suddenly a man was standing in front of my window and in a harsh voice ordered me to hang up the telephone. He appeared angry. He ordered me to step up to my door. He was associated with Rev. Colson's group whose initiates were "born again."

I supposed he was an official from the Bureau of Prisons.

I asked, "What do you want?"

He replied, "I'm a chaplain from the Prison Ministries." His voice was sharp. I was bewildered. He barked at me, "Do you want to speak to me?"

I said, politely, "No."

He moved on almost exactly how I would imagine a Prussian officer to move by.

While I was still studying Christianity at that time, I knew for certain I was opposed to all of these preachers. They *use* the Christian Bible as an instrument to attack everyone (not just non-Christians) with the "instinctual" confidence that when the going gets rough they can bully the moderate Christians into supporting them—for the simple reason that they thump on a Bible every time they open their foul mouths. They practice the threat of physical violence over meeker Christians.

What is amusing about this and similar remarks anyone might make in this vein is this: The Christians point to remarks like mine and pretend *this* is "Christian Persecution." They *rule* all of Europe and America (at the least) and have the gall to complain of being "persecuted" when someone points out their courts are unjust, their governments are oppressive, and their policemen abuse their prisoners. The Christians call the fact anyone would complain "persecution." Christianity is a psychological persecution complex.

And they do it with the "true Christian" trick—exactly the same trick the Marxists use when they say Stalin was not a "true Marxist."

At any rate, over this period I began to reflect on how it was possible that I could have been so utterly deceived, and I began a study of the history of ideas. The ideas of philosophy without exception led back to Greece, and Christianity had been the transmitting force of these ideas— "transforming" them from pagan sources.

When I read Norman Mailer's book *Ancient Evenings,* I began to meditate on the ancient world, and I sought out material about Egypt.

I could not understand the so-called "kerygma" of Jesus—the *understanding* the people had in the many episodes contained in the "gospels." I never understood the *culture* that Jesus would have been born into and lived in. At the time, I was still under the presuppositions of my early "education." I had no idea of the role of Judea in antiquity, no idea of Judaism, and no idea of the Jews. I knew an individual was Jewish the same way I knew an individual was Catholic or Protestant or Mormon.

But when the court at Springfield finally lifted the restraint, and I was sent to Marion Prison, I had begun to wonder about the *culture* of

Jesus. I learned of Josephus first, the Judean scholar (once Governor of Galilee) who was present at the destruction of the Second Temple in Jerusalem. He wrote two major books, both histories of the Jews (*The Antiquities* and *The Jewish Wars*).

For the first time I discovered the old Judean people. Then I received the books Buber wrote about the hasidim—and I learned of the existence of the *Zohar* ("The Book of Splendor"). I had no idea such traditions were attached to the Book of Genesis and the rest of the first five books of "the Bible." Through this work I began to understand the culture of the Judeans—and an intellectual tradition much higher than that of the Greeks (and the Chinese).

I became converted to Judaism and began reading the Talmud and Midrash Rabbah. I spent all of 1984 as best I could as an observant, Orthodox Jew. When I was born, my foreskin had no opening and I could not pass water for several painful days. I was rushed to the military base and was circumcised. So I was already circumcised when I converted to Judaism and could therefore keep the observances.

I began reading the scholars of Orthodox Judaism (the Rav in particular) and understood, at that time, religious Zionism—or *misunderstood,* I should say, because I mistook it for political Zionism. Then (lastly) I discovered the modern history of the Jews, and I was perplexed to discover that almost without exception all my friends outside prison had been Jews yet had not introduced me to Judaism. I came to learn they knew as little as I did about Judaism. They are all assimilated. I know more than they do today.

The more I learned, the more it shocked me and undermined my previous understanding of history and of European culture, and I wrote tirades of anti-Semitic outpourings to my Jewish friends.

But a vision had begun to emerge from my study of these religious texts, and this was the whole history of man and of the earth, and science vindicates it (not merely Velikovsky's theory of the reversal of the earth's poles).

Among the ancient Judeans, G-d was held in such high esteem his name was never uttered except by High Priests on solemn occasions. The tradition of learning (the sage tradition) was the highest there ever was or ever will be among human beings. The higher esoteric teaching, for example, was not taught until a man was wise and had reached the age of forty. It was the duty of the learned men to master all the sciences, all worldly knowledge, before teaching the oral account of the Torah. The "torah," before Moses, meant "the teaching." After Moses it referred to the first five books of "the Bible," not merely to the Ten Commandments.

Past Christian scholars have ignored these ancient texts, and the reason they ignored them was and is ignorance. A higher expression of culture is not immediately accessible to someone from a lower culture, and all past Christian scholars, therefore, where they did attempt to comprehend it (cf. Bauer) only succeeded in childishly misunderstanding it for emotional reasons (in the main) having to do with guilt.

The *culture* of Christianity had its source in the culture of the Jews. The disputes Jesus reportedly had with the Sadducees are disputes *the Jews* had with the Sadducees who did not represent the Jewish people at that point in time. A sage named Hillel directed similar complaints against the Sadducees—at least a generation before Jesus was born. I believe Akiva had similar thoughts after the Temple.

It is accepted that Christianity had its beginnings in the Essene sect, which came into existence long before Herod became king over Judea. From the internal evidence of the Christian Gospels, Jesus and at least one of his followers belonged to the Essene movement. There is also evidence of this in Christian apocryphal documents, including the Nag Hammadi scrolls attributed to the disciple Thomas and others.

All of the documents of Christianity, especially the entirety of the "New Testament," were written in Greek. None of the documents was written in Hebrew.

Christianity collected all the attitudes and codes of behavior that slaves had to observe naturally to be content with their condition and their abuse of one another. These were embellished with Greek metaphysical concepts—which were later formalized by Augustine of Hippo to transform a crime against sanity and reason into a rational system (using Aristotle's work *The Metaphysics*).

I have spent most of my life among people who are large physically and who enjoy a harsh environment. They like to live in cold regions and conquer the soil from the rocks. Physiologically as well as culturally they would fit the category of warrior. They experienced a warrior culture, or what remains of it. They are not the kind of people who could even imagine being dominated. They have strong attitudes toward outsiders and feel threatened by no one. So I can understand how the ideas of Christianity could amuse them to the point of accepting Christianity. What harm could it do? It could even be conceived by them as a kind of cultural *refinement*—since they were so big and uncontested in the world, so hardy with heavy animal spirits; they were *coarse* and they knew it. This is the only way I can possibly imagine Christianity could be accepted, for example, by the big Nordic or Germanic peoples. This is how their spirit was imprisoned.

My earliest experience of Christianity was of being persecuted by Christians, but the most decisive experience was the endlessly redundant hypocrisy these otherwise large, well-constituted animals could not avoid. Physiologically I was not fit for the meat and milk diet, and their environment was a dangerous hardship for me. Their traditions of brawling left me at a disadvantage. In other words, I was not fit to endure the hypocrisy the way they were.

Christianity for the Christian occupies certain parts of reality and denies the existence of other parts of reality. It defines taboos against things that are not supposed to be in the world. This is a *daemonic* understanding—and it does not matter if it appears with a kind, benevolent smile overflowing with pity and love. When humanity has rid itself of this poison, especially given the high degree of civilization we now enjoy, there will truly be a "kingdom of heaven" on earth.

Anyone who has read the Jewish "Old Testament" with care could not read the "New Testament" without losing patience and tearing it out of "the Bible."

The objective history of the land of Israel (Judea, Galilee, etc.) at the time of Herod—and a hundred years before him and after him—shows us a *people* so at odds with the *society* in the Gospels as to constitute itself a refutation of the Gospels. The world Jesus moved through in the Gospels most certainly was not Galilee and Judea. I could only place such a world in Greece, after the last Great Plague in which Pericles died. After the devastations, the *ruin,* their "son of god" among the insane and dying would have made sense. But not in Judea. Not in Galilee. The people were not only healthy and robust but had access to arts of medicine no other single civilization enjoyed at the time, including Rome. It was the only *literate nation* on earth at the time. Public education was an essential part of the national culture.

When I was younger I read all the Christian philosophers, from Augustine onward. And I read the Christian "existentialists" as well. Kierkegaard impressed me more by *pathesis,* by his poetical and intellectual literary flights, than by his knowledge. One example is the beautiful foolishness he "divined" about Don Juan and Father Abraham—not to mention Antigone and other Greek subjects.

I have read more than three hundred books from the time of my arrest in October 1981, to January 1986. Most of them were works on science (physics, the brain, and biology in particular), ancient languages, and archeological histories. I read again the texts of the major religions, including the Chinese religions, the Zoroasterian, the Moslem and the Hindu religions. Over a hundred of the texts were on the Jews.

Only the Torah contains a factual account of the origins of all people on earth from the beginning to all the branches of mankind. In all the other traditions, no mention is made of any other peoples except the peoples native to each particular religious cultural tradition. I am satisfied beyond a doubt that the culture of the Jews traces the culture of all of mankind, and the secret of mankind's separation from a prior condition of perfection (or "peace") is to be found in an enlightened comprehension of the ancient texts of Judaism.

Those who are in ignorance can master their emotions only when they come to the gates of this spiritual temple that is destined for the return of all mankind to itself and that lost condition of man he is now separated from.

Is *this* a religion? Are my conclusions a religion? The study of the oral account of the Torah refers me to the various branches of science, and I take pleasure in *knowing*—not in "faith" nor in "believing."

Nor do I agree with the idea that Communists are in possession of truth anymore than the Nazis. Marx and Engels pursued false paths by dialectical means, but a great deal of what Marx and Engels discovered was and still is valid.

It has always been the Jews who have been the bearers of the higher culture, who have brought scientific and moral enlightenment to the masses and broken down barriers to individual betterment. Stalin resisted this fact of history in his erroneous theory of "proletarian culture," seeing problems where none existed save for his own Georgian rural "culture."

Stalin betrayed the great historical *trust*.

Fraternally,
Jack

Postscript

It is said:

When Adam was exiled from the Garden of Eden, and he came forth into the world, he saw the days growing shorter and shorter.

He was stricken and his confusion was kindled. He thought the world was dying. He ran to and fro in the earth, trying to stop the world from dying.

Adam was wild with grief. Adam wept. Adam cried out.

It was only when the days began to grow longer that Adam began to grow calm. As the days lengthened his confusion subsided and he put away his grief. Adam realized there was a higher cycle governing and uniting the days and that the world was not dying.

Adam smiled.

Selah

ABOUT THE AUTHORS

Jack Henry Abbott has written reviews and articles and is the author of a book, *In the Belly of the Beast.* He is presently in prison in New York. He is forty-three years of age. Naomi Zack received her doctorate in philosophy at Columbia University, where she was awarded two Woodrow Wilson Fellowships and where she taught for a short period. She is a native of Manhattan and is forty-two years of age.